Planes and Pilots

CW01675019

FRENCH AIRCRAFT

1939 - 1942

Fighters, Bombers, Reconnaissance and Observation Types

TOME 1 : From Amiot to Curtiss

André JOUINEAU
Dominique BREFFORT

Translated from the French by Alan McKay

HISTOIRE & COLLECTIONS

Morane-Saulnier MS 406 from GC 1/7 photographed on the base at Rayak, Syria, during the spring of 1941. This squadron was the first to be equipped with this type of fighter from 1938 but did not take part in the Battle of France; its first combat experience was in 1942 against the... British who had become the new enemy at the time! *(ECPAD)*

FOREWORD

'Where are our planes?' How many times were these words been spoken, not only during the dramatic weeks of May and June 1940, but for a long time after the Battle of France? And yet, at the time, the Armée de l'Air did have planes and in particular it did have pilots who fought, who even fought well especially if you take into account the equipment they were using, that subtle blend of out-of-date and therefore vulnerable machines and new, modern aircraft with all their teething troubles which not always corrected.

Thanks to these two new volumes in our collection 'Planes and Pilots', we are going to try and present this dramatic period of the Armée de l'Air's history somewhat better and at the same time in our own way honour both those aces with many victories and all the anonymous actors who took part in this drama.

It is for this reason that this book and the following companion volume is a little out of the ordinary: it is not devoted to just one plane and its variants; on the contrary it is a general overview of the machines, either made in France or bought abroad and used by the Armée de l'Air between September 1939, when the Second World War started and November 1942 when French military aviation which the Armistice convention had finally authorised to continue was disbanded.

The subject is so wide that we had to fix limits so that we could get it all into the space available. For this reason this study has deliberately left out transports and trainers – or those used for training (whether they were designed for training from the outset, or out of date or reconverted fighters and bombers whose numbers and variety - especially the bombers - would have meant going beyond the possibilities of such a book as this which is naturally limited). The Aéronavale has not been dealt with either, both because of the lack of space and because it is in itself a separate subject, worthy of at least one book of this type. Finally at the end of each volume, still in alphabetical order, there is a little group of prototypes built and flying before the end of hostilities but which circumstances prevented from being produced in series, even though this was planned and indeed sometimes already started.

N.B. For reasons of simplicity we have chosen present the planes in alphabetical order; the planes are presented using their most common name even if this does not correspond to the one in the official texts. For example the MB 152 will be found under the more general name of 'Bloch', rather than the then more official name of SNCASO. Only machines taken on charge and tested by the Armée de l'Air are dealt with in this book, even if only a few were delivered. Machines which were ordered but never actually delivered, like the Curtiss H-81 - the future P-40, the Lockheed P-38, Consolidated B-24, etc., are only mentioned generally in the text.

FROM THE BIRTH OF THE ARMÉE DE L'AIR TO THE DISSOLUTION OF THE VICHY AIR FORCE

In November 1918, France had the world's strongest air force; twenty-one years later on the eve of WWII, it was in a much less enviable situation and paid very dearly for the procrastination, delays and other strategic mistakes which characterised the inter-war period. The first result of the end of the war had been the cancellation of most of the aircraft orders and the laying off of the greater part of the aircraft industry's workforce; things did not really change afterwards, especially where attitudes were concerned. It was this factor, combined with the serious mistakes made at the highest level of the armed forces which explain the defeat of the French Air Force at the beginning of the summer of 1940.

A Succession of Plans

It was only in 1922 that the French Air Force really became independent. An Air Ministry was set up six years later in September 1928. At the time, the French Air Force was called the 'Forces Aériennes de Terre' (Land Air Forces); this dependence on the Army was visible in the way the aircraft were allotted, the majority (60 %) going to observation and the rest split between the other functions, fighters getting 28 % and bombers 12 %.

It was in 1933 that Pierre Cot, the recently appointed Air Minister, created the Etat-Major Général des Forces Aériennes (Air Force General Staff), the term 'Armée de l'Air' being used here for the first time, even though it was only in July 1934 that it was really set up. It was given three essential tasks: to defend French air space, to fight for air superiority, and to cooperate with land and sea forces. A large programme to renovate and increase its means, called Plan I, was adopted in June 1933 and was intended to give French military aviation the benefit of the latest technical progress. Among the new machines concerned by this were the Dewoitine 500 and 501, the Amiot 140, the Bloch 200 and the ANF-Les Mureaux 117. The first part of this plan, which included the production of more than 1 000 machines per year, should in theory have been completed by 1 January 1936. In fact, this programme was never completed because of the inadequacy of French industry at that time; there were delays and some of the planes were out of date before even entering service. At the end of 1935, only 500 out of the 1 300 aircraft planned had been produced; this delay turned out to be a great handicap in the future since by preventing the Air Force from modernising obliged it to use planes which were in fact two years out of date. The initial objectives were therefore reviewed, the authorities being satisfied with putting in to service 1 150 out of the 1 500 aircraft originally planned. More seriously however as the fact that certain projects were launched using concepts which were often mistaken and which used just as much money as energy only to end up with failures, like the October 1933 BCR (Bombardement, Combat et Renseignement – Bombing, Combat and Reconnaissance) programme which was inspired by the theories of the Italian officer, General Giulio Douhet and which resulted in machines like the Potez

Opposite: **Morane Saulnier MS 405 in flight. The direct successor of this fighter, the MS 406, equipped a great deal of French *Groupes de Chasse* at the beginning of WW2, in September 1939.** *(Archives WM).*

Above:, **The MB 152 production line at the SNCASO factory at Châteauroux-Déols. In a few years French aircraft manufacturers progressed from the workshop to the mass-production stage, not without difficulties.** *(Coll. J. Delmas)*

As French aircraft manufacturers were not able to supply the aircraft by the set dates, foreign help was brought in, especially from the USA. Here the Curtiss H-75 A-1 N°4 rolling out, shipped by sea and assembled at Bourges by the SNCAC. *(Coll. J. Delmas)*

Above:
The Morane-Saulnier factory in which some of the 1 000 MS 406s were made; this was a considerable number given the embryonic state of the French aircraft industry at the beginning of the thirties. *(Archives WM)*

540 and Bloch 131 which very quickly proved to be incapable of even carrying out even one of the three tasks they were intended for properly. This situation caused a new five-year plan to be adopted during the summer of 1936 which concerned among others the MS 405 and the Bloch 131. But even before they were reached, these targets were again called into question and the plan abandoned less than a year later. After the re-militarization of the Rhineland, a new programme was launched in September 1936 under the title 'Plan II' or 'Plan des 1 500' (the 1 500 Plan). It was intended to cover the period 1937 to 1940 and favoured the bomber units which were in a deplorable condition; it introduced new types of aircraft such as the Morane-Saulnier 405-406 and the future Potez 63 family. Plan II suffered from countless delays, so much so that planes intended for 1932 and which had been allowed for in the plan only came off the production lines in 1938, delayed even further by nationalisations following the arrival of the Front Populaire Government which came to power in 1936.Up to the declaration of war, these large-scale programmes followed one after another, starting with Plan III which was to reinforce the anti-aircraft defences and to develop fighters; but it was never launched. The 1937 Plan IV which planned to modernise reconnaissance aircraft was finally thrown out before it was even started; the whole of the rearmament programme for the Armée de l'Air was thus held back. As the international situation went from bad to worse, particularly after the Anschluss, Germany's annexation of Austria, a Plan V was adopted in March 1938 whose main objective was to ensure the protection of French Territory and the rest of the Empire, first by building up a greater offensive potential together with Great Britain than Germany had with Italy, France's target being to equal the might of Germany. By the planned date, 4 739 war machines, among which there were some new types (MS 406, Bloch 152 and D. 520, in particular), were to have been produced; the assault category of aircraft appeared on the scene with the Breguet 690 series and series production of the LeO 45 and Amiot 350 was also planned.

This Plan V was reviewed and reinforced several times, especially in June 1939; it was intended to bring the strength up to 8 000 combat aircraft by the end of the same year. The reality was entirely different because at the end of the first stage of the programme only 527 of the planned 1 878 aircraft had been built. The Air Force's technical delay could not be made up quickly and with war looming closer every day, it was decided to resort to foreign help, mainly the United States. Various types (such as the Curtiss H-75, Douglas DB-7, Glenn Martin 167, North American NAA 57 and 64, etc.) were ordered for fighter, bomber and training units.

When war broke out on 3 September 1939, the French Air Force had just started to recover and only had slightly more than 1 400 machines which could be called 'modern' (MS 406, Potez 63 and variants, Bloch 131, 151 and 152, Curtiss H-75, Breguet 691, Farman 224, LeO 451, etc.) at its disposal, of which only 500 were really capable of doing anything; this was even though the reinforced Plan V had intended there to be 1 730 planes by that date. Of the 23 existing fighter units, 19 were equipped with modern aircraft but there were still some fighters with out-of-date performances such as the Dewoitine 500/510 and the Spad 510 still in service. The bomber units were in an even sorrier state with their slow, cumbersome, and therefore very vulnerable, Bloch 200/210s and Amiot 143s; the observation units were still the poor relations of the Air

The Arsenal VG-33, which originated with the fighters built with non-strategic materials programme, was a very promising aircraft. Unfortunately only a handful of them came off the production lines before the end of hostilities. This is prototype n° 01. (SHAA)

Above: **Although it was way out-of-date at the beginning of the war, the MB 200 equipped several bomber squadrons in Metropolitan France and overseas when hostilities started; not all of them had been replaced by the beginning of the German onslaught on 10 May 1940...** *(Coll. J. Delmas)*

Above, right: **The MB 174 (here N° 27) was without doubt one of the best French planes of the Battle of France, but it arrived too late and in too few numbers to influence the outcome of the fighting.** *(SHAA)*

Force, as they had always been; the crews had to make up for the failings of the outmoded Mureaux and Potez 25s with their skill and courage... When hostilities began, France possessed 7450 machines (to which must be added those belonging to the *Aéronavale*, the Navy Air Arm); more precisely this meant 3959 combat aircraft of which 3697 were based in France itself and in North Africa. But out of this number more than 1000 aircraft (1104 to be precise) were considered as 'ancient' or even 'very ancient' (LeO 20/206, Potez 25 etc.) and 1570 were considered to be 'transitional' types (the Amiot 143, MB 200 and 210 etc.).

The Phoney War

Although on the ground the military situation remained relatively calm during the first eight months of the war, operations in the air started to intensify as of the second week of hostilities. The Air Force was entrusted with watching the Siegfried Line and undertook strategic reconnaissance missions over the Saar. The first dogfight (an MS 406 versus an Me 109) took place on 8 September 1939; September was the most deadly month of the Phoney War since the Air Force lost 30 aircraft during this period. The situation got worse when Poland, whom some people had thought would resist for a year, was brushed aside in three weeks with Germany being able to send its elite units (equipped with the Messerschmitt Bf 109) back to the west. Modernising the Air Force became vital and a 'War Plan V' was put into operation on 14 September.

It planned to line up 3200 planes in combat order – for this reason it was sometimes called the '3200 Plan' - at the same time building up reserves, a total of 6500 planes. The time limit was fixed for the beginning of April 1940. In reality, once again, the result was a far cry from the initial forecasts; only the fighters were anywhere near ready, with 2138 out of the planned 2960 aircraft coming off the assembly lines before the date limits. The bomber units were once again the least well equipped with only 280 out of the 1940 aircraft planned received by the units. The reconnaissance units had received half of their quota of planes and the modernisation and the reinforcement of the transport units were almost non-exis-

Opposite:
Several bomber groups were still equipped with the Amiot 143 right up until the June 1940 Armistice; conversions onto other aircraft were never completed or even carried out. In spite of their great vulnerability, these truly flying dinosaurs did not suffer too many losses as they were very quickly used less to limit the risks... Here N° 94 shot down by the Flak over Mainz, on 15 October 1939. (ECPAD)

Above: **The best fighter in the French arsenal was the Dewoitine D.520 (here the second prototype), but there were delays before a number – in the end quite insufficient - of fighter squadrons were supplied with this aircraft.** *(Coll. J. Delmas)*

The development of camouflage and markings (1939-1942)

Up until the Munich Crisis in the summer of 1938, all French fighters were natural metal colour (with a protective varnish coat) and bombers were 'tableau green' or brown (called 'chocolat' or 'tête de nègre'), their engine cowlings were metal coloured. The large-sized unit insignia were worn on the fuselage, like the roundels on the lower and upper wing surfaces which had to be 90 % of the wing's chord at the tips.

On **6 December 1938** (Instruction N°1422), multi-coloured camouflage appeared ; new machines were factory-camouflaged, the others were camouflaged gradually in the units. The upper surfaces and the sides were painted khaki and the underneath in light grey-blue ; the limit between the two shades, on the flanks and the leading edges, had to be blurred. These two basic colours had to be mixed with green, burnt umber, natural sienna, white, black and even red and blue in order to obtain the dark hues applied in large patches which were shaded off and which had no particular geometrical shape. In reality the planes which were already in service started by being simply painted khaki and light blue, the patches of colours starting to appear gradually during 1939. The new

planes were given a basic coat of khaki or dark grey-blue over which brown and grey-blue patches or brown and khaki (depending on the background colour) were painted. As a general rule, these shades were applied without a particular pattern (only a few types, like the Bloch 174 or the LeO 451 seemed to have had more regular patterns applied) the shades themselves varying considerably since they were usually obtained by mixing the colours. The underside roundels were reduced in size to measure only 12 inches across and the size of the upper roundels corresponded to 4/5ths of the wing chord. It was thus that French aircraft entezed the war in September 1939.
In January 1940 the upper roundels were enlarged (diameter more than 4 feet)

and a roundel measuring 2 ft 7 in was added to the fuselage sides, not always exactly in the same place. The flight insignia had to be painted (smaller : 12 in by 12 in) on the tail fin, the individual number of the plane being painted on the fuselage behind the roundel (in the direction of flight). Finally, the 'Matricule militaire' (registration number) was no longer painted on new planes.
On **9 July 1940**, after the Armistice signed a few days earlier, the fuselage roundel (2 ft across) was given a white 2-in wide border and the wing roundels were reduced to 2 ft 7 in across. A white 4-in wide stripe had to be added along the

fuselage but its length was not specified. All planes including the Aéronautique Navale were given this stripe but in this case it was only painted through the roundel. From **May 1941** onwards, French planes which were to be engaged in Syria had their tails and engine cowlings up to the wing leading edges painted yellow.
On **24 June 1941**, alternating yellow and red stripes (8 to 10 inches wide) had to be painted over the whole tail surface (except for the tricolour rudder which did not change), the front part of the engine cowlings and if possible on the part between the rear of the engines and the level of the leading edges. These were commonly called the 'Vichy Stripes'. The roundels on the wings had to be 31 inches across and those on the fuselage 24 inches. The fuselage stripe was kept and had to extend beyond the roundel by at least 5 ft 3 in.
In a directive dated **13 December 1941** which was extended to all the planes in the Armée de l'Air by a rectification dated **6 February 1942** tricolour stripes

converging forwards at 30° to the longitudinal axis of the machine and 1 foot wide had to be painted on the wings, together with the preceding markings ; the roundel and the white line on the fuselage were removed. From now on, only aircraft painted in this way were authorised to fly.
In Indochina, a note dated **9 February 1942** obliged planes flying in that zone to bear a 4-inch wide white stripe on the rear of the fuselage with the whole of the tail painted red.
After **14 November 1942** and the invasion of the so-called 'Unoccupied Zone' of France by the Germans, the rare planes allowed to fly during the brief period before the dissolution of the Armée de l'Air had to wear white 'scarves'

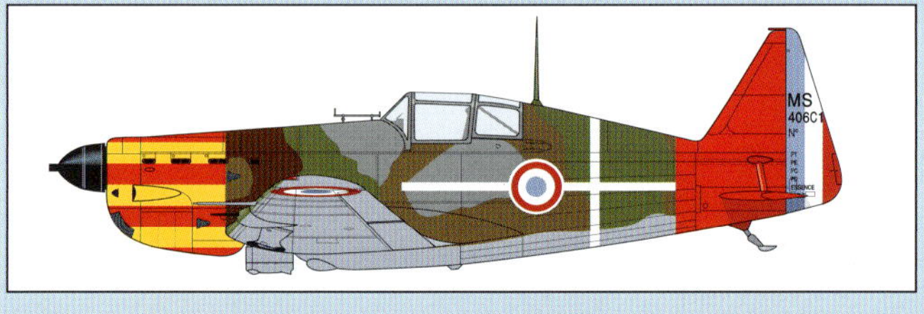

(a 20-inch wide white stripe) round the wings and the fuselage, and between the engines and the end of the wings for twin-engined aircraft ; the upper surface of the engine cowlings remained red. ●

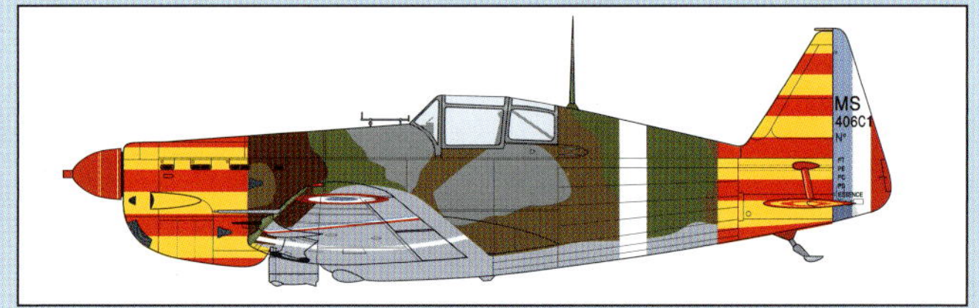

Opposite:
The Potez 63.11 (here N° 373, fitted with two-blade ferrying propellers, abandoned and being examined by the Germans) equipped most of the GAOs and paid a heavy tribute during the fighting in the Battle of France, despite the great courage of the crews. *(Coll. S. Bonneau).*

tent. Since 'War Plan V' was, as we have just seen, yet another failure, and since Plan Vbis of February 1940 had not had the chance even to get off the ground, another plan, Plan VI, was put into operation in April 1940 onwards.

More than 3500 front line aircraft had to be supplied to the Armée de l'Air (1 770 fighters, 732 bombers and 1 032 reconnaissance planes) so that by April 1941 it would possess 9200 aircraft thus equipping 50 single-seat fighter groups, 10 multi-seater fighter groups, five night-fighter groups, 22 bomber groups (medium and heavy), 16 assault bomber groups, 15 reconnaissance groups, 60 observation groups. The dive-bomber category was left out entirely. Once again because the war gathered speed and the German attacked in May, this last plan was never put into operation...

Although on the ground there was not much going on, during the first months of the conflict, the French nevertheless lost 124 machines against 77 (or 74) German aircraft for a number of missions which was actually quite high: 9500 for the fighter units and 2000 for the reconnaissance units.

The Battle of France (May-June 1940)

Even if it is true that the initial programmes were only partly completed, the Armée de l'Air was undoubtedly modernised during the Phoney War and was therefore in a better state in May 1940 than at the beginning of the war. It was particularly quality which had improved, the most outmoded fighters being gradually replaced by newer types, and Fighter Squadrons (made up of 26 planes) equipped with MS 406s were less numerous than at the beginning of the war. Only GC 1/3 however used the top performance Dewoitine D.520, whereas the Arsenal VG.33, the 'third generation' fighter was not even in the order of battle...

Before the 10 May and the Battle of France, there were 637 fighters (of which 570 single-seaters) based in Metropolitan France; the reconnaissance units were mainly equipped with the Potez 63-11 (35 *Groupes Aériens d'Observation* or GAO out of 46), and the MB 174s were only inventoried in very small numbers. Thus the Armée de l'Air only had 1394 front line planes, to which were added the trainers, the depot and reserve machines, together with the 416 British planes in the Air Component of the AASF (Advanced Air Striking Force) and the contribution of the Belgian and Dutch air forces (about 300 planes). If all these machines are added together a total figure of 3200 planes is obtained with which to confront the 4000 front line Luftwaffe aircraft (some sources even give 4300 planes) shared out between two *Luftflotten*.

Above:
If the Bloch 131 (top) was retired from the front lines, the MB 210 together with the Amiot 143 was the backbone of the French bomber force; some of them still served in their groups at the time of the Battle of France. *(Archives WM)*

Following the German 'Yellow Plan', which provided for the Luftwaffe's destruction of French, Belgian and Dutch aerodromes and aircraft, as well as the railway network linking the East to the Champagne and Soissons areas, 72 air bases were attacked by 400 aircraft on the morning of 10 May, causing the loss of some dozens of French aircraft, mostly destroyed on the ground; in Belgium and Holland the destruction was far more serious; the *Luchtvaartafdeling*, the Dutch Air Force, was destroyed during the first day of the onslaught. Meanwhile, the Armée de l'Air was not inactive and carried out 360 sorties on the first day during which 44 enemy aircraft were shot down for a loss of 24 planes. Even though on the evening of the first day of the fighting, the French had lost 53 machines

After the Armistice, two assault squadrons were kept which flew Breguet 693/695s until they were disbanded. Here Br 695 N°8 from GBA II/51 in 1942. *(SHAA)*

destroyed on the ground and 14 in dogfights, the Armée de l'Air was a long way off being out of action, as history would too often have us believe. The allied armies established in Northern France penetrated into Belgium and some machines from the French Groupes de Chasse even carried out missions over Dutch territory. On 11 May the Germans reached the Albert Canal and the River Maas which the French tried in vain to stop them crossing by launching truly suicide missions, like those carried out by the Breguet 693s on 12 May. On 13 May, the Germans threw seven armoured divisions at the linchpin between the troops which had moved up into Belgium and the French land units situated in the East; about 2000 tanks drove in the front in three places: Dinant, Monthermé and Sedan. These troops penetrated the French lines right to the rear and in depth. The Armée de l'Air tried to oppose the Panzers which were very effectively backed up by their air force. The land forces had to be supported at all costs and with all means available, which meant that the Lower Seine region was drained of its cover. On 14 May, the Germans crossed the Maas (Meuse) and the following day, the IX Army was pierced. On 16 May the Air Force bases were threatened and General Vuillemin planned to fall back.

On 17 May, the bombing missions which had been planned initially were cancelled enabling the various units to regroup and reorganise. On the following day, the order was given to operate as close to the front as possible so as to save on materiel as much as possible since the potential strength of the *Groupes de Chasse* (Fighter Squadrons) and *Groupes de Bombardement* (Bomber Squadrons) had been seriously depleted; training aircraft and armed training centre aircraft were thrown into the fray. In less then eight days, the Wehrmacht had driven the allied armies to the North Sea, the Channel and Abbeville being reached on 20 May; the Panzers even had to slow down in order not to leave the motorised units behind.

On 21 May the Germans set up a bridgehead to the south of Amiens and two days later, the *Groupe d'Armées Nord* was caught up in the noose in Flanders and Belgium which capitulated on 28 May. On the same day Operation 'Dynamo' started; this was the evacuation of the encircled troops (about 340000 men) in the Dunkirk pocket; this operation ended on 2 June.

The hardest air battle of the whole campaign took place on 3 June, when Paris was attacked by the Luftwaffe which used 200 bombers and 150 fighters. 13 French (with the Poles of GC 1/145) lost their lives for a total of 19 kills of which 6 were probables. During the following days, the situation got worse and worse and when the Germans launched the second phase of their offensive on 5 June, the real Battle of France began. All units were given the order to defend their positions at all costs, but the offensive front formed by the French along the Rivers Somme and Aisne was driven in: the Seine was reached on the 9th, Rouen was taken on the following day. Nothing seemed to be able to halt the Panzers...

Faced with this flood (in two weeks German armour, starting on the Aisne, had pushed beyond Besançon and Lyon), French units were forced to fall back further each day, literally chased out of their bases by the German motorised units, very effectively supported by the Luftwaffe. The squadrons changed aerodromes every day, and planes started to pile up on the ever diminishing number of airfields. As of 12 June, the day Rheims fell, the idea of an armistice was already being suggested. On the ground there was total confusion, GHQ's decisions were more and more contradictory, even despairing; the situation was worsened by the fact that the reconnaissance aircraft even though indispensable had been wiped out and their missions had to be carried out by other air Force units.

On 10 June, a second front was opened with Italy's entry into the war, hostilities really starting on the night of 12 to 13 June with the bombing of the St Tropez torpedo factory. On 14 June, Paris was declared an 'open city'; it then fell; the transfer of aircraft to French North Africa was organised and only night bombing missions on very precise targets were kept up. Britain got most of its units out leaving only five fighter squadrons on the other side of the Channel. When the Armistice was signed on 22 June 1940, the Armée de l'Air

A group of pilots from GC II/9 poses in front of an MB 152 in 1941. *(ECPAD)*

Above: **MS 406s lining up at the Ecole de l'Air at Salon-de-Provence in 1942. The Roman figures on the second plane perhaps indicate that it had been assigned to GC I/2 at some time.** *(ECPAD)*

claimed to have shot down 733 enemy aircraft for a loss of 852 machines (504 fighters, 211 bombers and 137 observation and reconnaissance aircraft). 500 French pilots had been killed wounded or listed as missing - about 20 % of the officers and 15 % of the flying NCOs.

On the Side of the Axis

Because of the defeat (the heaviest that the French Armed Forces had ever suffered in the whole of its history), the French authorities were in no real position to negotiate the terms of the Armistice with the victors; these turned out to be particularly severe for the Air Force: at first the Germans demanded that it be completely disbanded. All machines had to be handed over to the victors or stocked after being dismantled... The possible reconstitution of an Air Force was planned, to take place when a peace agreement had been signed, although the new air power was in no way to be of any threat to the victors' security. With this in view, flights were banned after 25 June, the day the armistice was to go into effect; this was intended to prevent men fleeing and rallying Great Britain; the demobilisation plan was to be completed by 15 September 1940.

Apart from the intervention of General Bergeret, it was the British attack on the French Fleet at Mers-el-Kebir (3 July 1940) which had a decisive effect on French military aviation, even though the intervention of the Armée de l'Air during this operation was rather symbolic (the fighter units had to get their aircraft airworthy after the tyres had been deflated and the propellers removed - to prevent any escape attempts - before being able to intervene in the fight). As a result, the one-sided clauses were rapidly suspended and demobilisation put off sine die, mainly so that the Armée de l'Air could react to possible attacks of this sort.

An 'Armistice Air Force' was therefore organised, closely supervised by the victors who limited its strength and equipment. Slightly fewer than 350 machines, shared out among eight fighter squadrons, six bomber squadrons and three reconnaissance squadrons, were kept in Metropolitan France in order to protect the 'Unoccupied Zone', and several units were stationed overseas (the Levant, French North, Eastern and Western Africa, Madagascar and French Indochina). A number of aircraft types were retired, leaving mainly the most modern types (D 520, LeO 451, MB 155, DB-7, Glenn Martin 167F (aka Maryland), although the Amiot 143 was also kept). Men and equipment were reduced quite a lot and aerodromes and airfields were controlled by Italian and German commissions. The number of flying hours was also very strictly controlled even though there were substantial differences depending on where units were situated; the quotas for overseas-based units were higher because of the number of aircraft transferred before hostilities ceased, there being about 630 machines in French North Africa.

The decision to maintain the French Air Force operational seemed to be justified when, a few weeks later, it turned upon its former ally, the United Kingdom and even its brothers-at-arms fighting with the Free French Forces, during Operation 'Menace', the attempt to capture Dakar by the British and the FFL on 23 September 1940. This attack failed mainly because of the Armée de l'Air's intervention and reprisal raids were even carried out against Gibraltar during the following two days, but these were Vichy's last offensive missions. It was in particular the Syrian Campaign (May to July 1943), which was the main confrontation in which the French State's (Vichy) Air Force took part. Despite the successes (29 confirmed kills and eight probables, but 179 planes lost – mainly destroyed on the ground – out of 279 committed), the fighting showed how weak this air force really was and how cruelly it lacked new and modern aircraft (the D 520s were worn out and were not up to the P-40s when these arrived); it also lacked specialised personnel, mainly through lack of training. The Vichy Air Force played a minor role during the fighting in Madagascar in May 1942 and finally, the following November, during Operation 'Torch' (the Allied landings in North Africa) when it experienced its most violent fighting.

At the time there were still about 600 machines left in service in French North Africa which suffered heavy losses (470 planes destroyed, again mainly on the ground) but not without causing the invaders quite heavy losses. This fighting was the last opportunity for Vichy's Air Force to show itself since the ceasefire signed on 10 November was followed by the invasion of the 'Unoccupied Zone' which had been 'free' until then; the 'Armistice Air Force' was disbanded on the 27th of the same month, at least in theory since an anti-aircraft unit continued to operate a few more months in Metropolitan France. Meanwhile on the other side of the Mediterranean, the Armée de l'Air was recreated with the help of American and English equipment and got ready to fight alongside the Allies, particularly in Metropolitan France, from mid-1944 onwards.

But that, as they say, is another story...

AMIOT 143

Above: **Amiot 143 N°42 of the 3e *Escadrille* of GB II/35 with the insignia of the 35e *Escadre de Bombardement* on the fuselage. This full profile shot also shows the form of the glazing preceding the definitive version.** *(ECPAD)*

It was with an official note from the French Air Ministry dating from the beginning of 1928, that the story of the Amiot 143M began. This document in effect required a 'multi-seat' combat plane capable of carrying out day and night bombing missions. Four builders took part in the competition: Blériot, Breguet, the SPCA (the Société Provençale de Construction Aéronautique) and the SECM (the Société d'Emboutissage et de Construction Mécanique) run by Félix Amiot who presented a machine designated 140M (M for *multiplace* - multi-seat) of which two prototypes were built. The first (01) was originally to be powered by two liquid-cooled Lorraine 18s but was finally fitted with Hispano-Suiza 12 Nbrs engines and flew for the first time on 12 April 1931, winning the competition in the end. The second (n° 02) was fitted with Lorraine engines but never took to the air.

Some modifications were made after the first trials, such as adding a front turret, moving the bomb bay to the left and enlarging the windows of the gondola. The machine thus modified was known as the Amiot 141M but it bore no offspring.

As production had been officially accepted in November 1933 and an order for 40 machines rapidly placed, two prototypes were therefore ordered, the Amiot 142, powered by two liquid-cooled Hispano-Suiza 12 Ybrs and the Amiot 143 with two air-cooled Gnôme-Rhône 14K Mistral Majors. The Amiot 143 prototype took off for the first time on 1 August 1934 powered by a 740 bhp Gnôme-Rhône 14 Kars on the port and a 14 Kbrs on the starboard side.

A short while later it was given 850 bhp 14 Kirs/Kjrs engines. The three blade propellers also made by Gnôme-Rhône had variable pitch (but this was adjusted on the ground only) and turned in opposite directions in order to avoid excessive yawing in case one of the engines broke down. Several modifications were made after the first official trials carried out at the CEMA (*Centre d'Expérimentation du Matériel Aérien* (*) - Air Equipment Experimentation Centre) including enlarging the tail and reinforcing the fuselage (September 1934), lengthening the engine nacelles by 10 inches (December 1934) and installing new turrets (January 1935). It was only in February 1935 that the Amiot 142 N°01 flew for the first time first fitted with Hispano- Suiza 12Ys then 14 Has power plants. This machine was finally refitted with Gnôme-Rhône engines and became the Amiot 143 N°75, the liquid-cooled engines being reserved for the fighters; the version of the 140 equipped with the liquid-cooled engines was finally abandoned. The first machine of the production series flew for the first time in April 1935, a year after the initially planned delivery date. Two further contracts for 73 and 25 machines respectively were signed in April 1935 and in 1936. In all 148 Amiot 143Ms were produced, the last being delivered in March 1937. This twin-engined aircraft was entirely made of metal; its wing was placed high on the fuselage and covered with Duralumin and was so thick that the engines and external reservoirs were accessible in flight by means of a tunnel installed within the internal structure. The fuselage had a rectangular cross-section and included a vast glazed two-level cockpit; the pilot occupied the upper part. The plane had fixed undercarriage and the wings had no flaps. The decision to use the plane for night bombing meant that a fifth crew member had to be accommodated; the crew finally consisted of pilot, co-pilot/navigator/bombardier, front and rear machine gunners and radio operator who also manned the lower defensive machine gun.

Originally designated Amiot 143MBN4, it became the B5 - for five-seat bomber. The bomb bay was offset towards the right in the vast glazed ventral gondola (a left-over from the inter-war days when the concept of the 'air cruiser' was still in fashion); there was a walkway and the bomb bay could contain a range of different loads: four 220-lb or 441-lb bombs on Type S racks, or 16 110-lb bombs on a TypeD8 rack or again 64 22-lb projectiles on two Type D32 racks. The offensive load could be increased by adding external pylons under each wing between the engine nacelles and the fuselage.

The defensive armament of the first 40 machines consisted of one.303 Lewis machine gun installed in the front To 23 turret, two others in the To 14bis dorsal turret and a further two on a semi-circular runner at the rear of the ventral gondola. The wing tanks could be jettisoned in flight. From the 41st example onwards, the Lewis guns were replaced by 7.5-mm MAC 34s, and the twin guns replaced by a single weapon.

Another machine gun was added on a flexible Type 29 mount firing through one of the panels in the front of the gondola. Finally the long-wave radios were replaced by Bronzavia short-wave sets. A structural modification was carried out from No 31 onwards by lengthening the fuselage by about a foot and the total length of the aircraft increased from 59 to 60 feet. The shape and position of the glazing were

(*) Cf. Glossary and abbreviations page 82.

Above: **Amiot N°16 (Reg. N° E-175) from the 3^e *Escadrille* of GB II/22. This squadron exchanged its Amiot 143s for MB 131s in September 1938. This plane was part of the first series of Amiot 143s up to N° 30 which were shorter by about a foot and which had different glazing.** *(Coll. J. Delmas)*

also touched up and the diameter of the front turret was increased.

Among the variants and derivatives of the Amiot 143, it is worth mentioning the Amiot 144M5 with a reduced wing area, fitted with flaps and retractable undercarriage but without its front turret. Based on the concept of the 'Combat Multi-seater', the only example of this machine flew on 18 January 1938 but the whole programme was finally abandoned at the end of the same year. As for the Amiot 145 and 146, they were nothing but Amiot 144s powered by Hispano-Suiza 14A4s or 1 100 bhp Gnôme-Rhône 18 Lars engines.

Neither of these machines was ever built. On the other hand, the Amiot 147 derived from the 144 and powered by liquid-cooled 880 bhp Hispano-Suiza 12 Ydrs/frs engines was tried out in October 1938 although there was no resulting production series. Finally the Amiot 150BE (for '*Bombardement Exploration*' – bombing and exploring) was identical to the production series machines except for a 10% bigger wing, and could be fitted with floats, as it was intended for use with the Aéronavale. The only example of this variant flew at Cherbourg but finished its career in an accident which occurred on 3 June 1939; it was never repaired.

The first *Groupe de Bombardement* to be equipped with the Amiot 143 was GB III/22 based at Chartres and which received its first machines in September 1935 before becoming GB II/22 in the following December. It was followed by GB I/22 in January 1936. GB III/12 based at Mourmelon was in turn converted in October 1936 and at the end of the same year, 72 machines were in the front line, with a dozen in reserve. Then it was the turn of the 34^e, 35^e and 38^e *Escadres* (Wings) of which GB I/38 received the machines which had been given to the 22nd Wing in September 1938; II/38 was also equipped with the Amiot 143 in March 1939 and II/63 stationed at Marrakech (Morocco) in the following spring. Although the 1937 Plan V had provided for the type to be retired from service, together with the Bloch 210, the Amiot 143 still formed the main structure of the French bomber force at the outbreak of war and equipped GB I/34 (based at Abbeville), II/34 (Poix), II/35 (Pontarlier) in France as well as GB I/38 and II/38 at Sétif in Tunisia. During the Phoney War, their missions were often limited to photographic reconnaissance and leaflet-dropping (a billion were dropped!) over enemy territory, their first action occurring on 15 September when two machines from GB II/34 carried out a reconnaissance mission. In order to reinforce the military position, two squadrons (GBs I/38 and II/38) flew in to France from Tunisia in October 1939.

At the beginning of the Battle of France, all these units were operational except for GB II/35 which had converted to Breguet 693 and which had given its machines to GB I/38 and II/38, and for GB II/63 which had converted to Glenn Martin 167F. In all 87 machines were in service, of which 50 in four squadrons (GB I/34 and II/34, and I/38 and II/38) in Metropolitan France and 17 in French North Africa. Because these machines were so vulnerable, nearly all the missions were carried out at night except for that of 14 May during which all machines were mobilised for the attack against the Germans crossing the Meuse at Sedan. Supported by LeO 451s, 19 Amiot (nine from I/34 and II/34 and ten from GB I/38 and II/38) were engaged; those from GB I/38 and II/38, not having found their escorting MS 406s turned back

Opposite: **In order to be up to strength, GB II/34 received a certain number of planes from bombing training centres (CIBs). These machines, like the one in the foreground (the unusable N°16 which now bears the number '8', just like the plane behind it, curiously enough), kept the characteristic markings of the training aircraft (white diagonal stripes) before being camouflaged.** *(DR)*

Above:
On this other shot of Amiot 143 N°16 (Reg. N° E-175) from GB II/22, part of the insignia painted on the tail can be seen - a stylised eagle seen sideways on - which was to be found again on the Potez 63.11 of GR II/22 because the unit was converted onto Potez.
(Coll. J. Delmas)

before reaching the target. Although three machines were lost (shot down or damaged beyond repair), it was not the massacre which is often described; it was in fact the RAF which was hardest hit on that particular day. Despite its slow speed and inadequate armament, the Amiot 143 was one of the least hit machines during the Battle of France, precisely because it carried out mainly night missions which were rightly considered less dangerous. After the Armistice, 52 Amiot 143s found themselves in the Unoccupied Zone and 25 in French North Africa, some machines having already been transferred abroad after 20 June. These bombers were regrouped at Istres in GBs I/38 and II/38, the only units maintained after the dissolution of *Groupement 34* in August 1940; they continued using these machines until July 1941, when they were converted to the LeO 451.

During the Syrian Campaign (May-July 1941), a *Groupe de Marche* was made up with some machines from GB II/38; then the Amiot 143 became a transport aircraft, especially within the 3^{e} *Escadrille* (3rd Flight) of GT I/15, which became III/15 and was sent from Istres to Oujda (Morocco) at the beginning of 1942. After the Allied landings in French North Africa (November 1942), this group went over to the allies and was given over to logistics support before becoming GT I/36 in January 1943. When the Germans occupied the Unoccupied Zone, there were only 11 planes left in France, three of which in flying condition. The Amiot 143s on the other side of the Mediterranean were used until the German defeat, sometimes for less glorious missions such as spraying insecticide over infected areas; the last plane was retired from Service in February 1944.

Opposite:
A crew in flying gear with leather helmets is loading bombs aboard an Amiot 143 whose wheels have had their spats removed; this was often done to prevent the wheels from blocking; this did not really penalise a plane that was already very slow!
(IWM)

TECHNICAL SPECIFICATIONS

Type
Multi-seat Bomber (5 men)

Power plant
Two 14-cylinder Gnôme-Rhône 14 Kirs (port), Kjrs (starboard) Mistral Major liquid-cooled radial engines developing 870 bhp.

Dimensions
Length: *60 ft 1 in.*
Height: *18 ft 7 in.*
Wingspan: *80 ft 7 in.*
Wing Area: *1 076.300 sq. ft.*
Weight Empty: *13,420 lb.*
Weight (Max.): *21,312 lb.*

Performance
Max. Speed: *194 mph at 13,200 feet.*
Range: *750 miles (max.: 1246 miles)*
Practical Ceiling: *26,070 feet.*

Armament
Four 7.5-mm MAC 34 machine guns: one in the front turret (800 rounds), one in the dorsal turret (1 200 rounds), one in the front of the ventral gondola (600 rounds) and one in the rear on a flexible mount (1 200 rounds). Offensive load of 1 936 lb to 3 520 lb in various combinations in the bomb bay or on underwing pylons.

Amiot 143

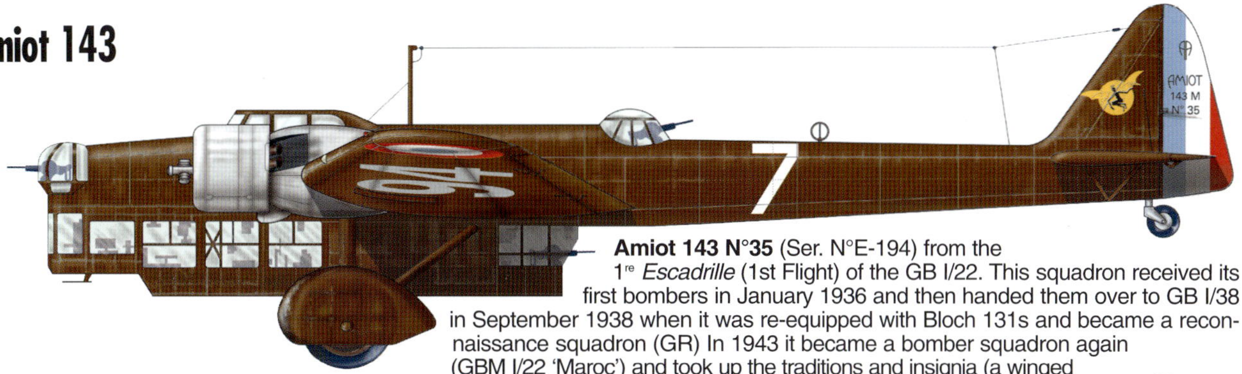

Amiot 143 N°35 (Ser. N°E-194) from the 1re *Escadrille* (1st Flight) of the GB I/22. This squadron received its first bombers in January 1936 and then handed them over to GB I/38 in September 1938 when it was re-equipped with Bloch 131s and became a reconnaissance squadron (GR) In 1943 it became a bomber squadron again (GBM I/22 'Maroc') and took up the traditions and insignia (a winged devil holding a bomb) of VB 109 which went back to 1915.

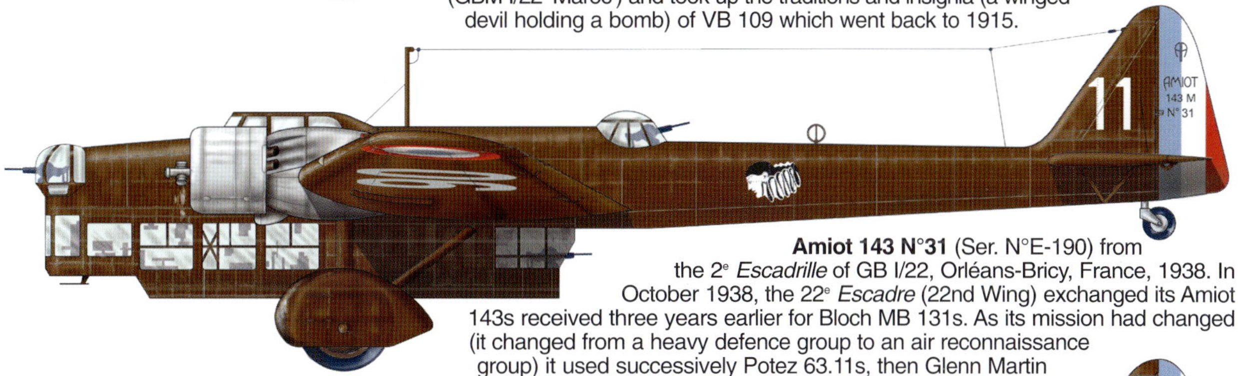

Amiot 143 N°31 (Ser. N°E-190) from the 2e *Escadrille* of GB I/22, Orléans-Bricy, France, 1938. In October 1938, the 22e *Escadre* (22nd Wing) exchanged its Amiot 143s received three years earlier for Bloch MB 131s. As its mission had changed (it changed from a heavy defence group to an air reconnaissance group) it used successively Potez 63.11s, then Glenn Martin 167Fs and LeO 451s.

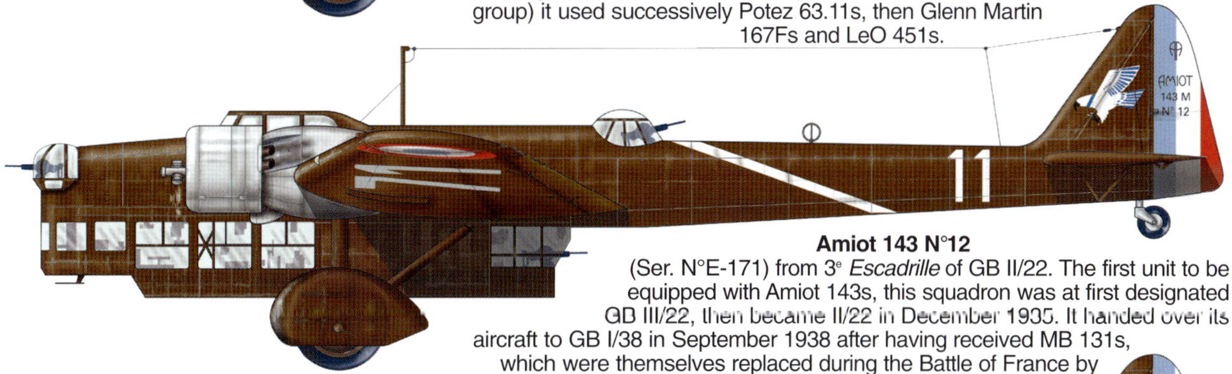

Amiot 143 N°12 (Ser. N°E-171) from 3^{e} *Escadrille* of GB II/22. The first unit to be equipped with Amiot 143s, this squadron was at first designated GB III/22, then became II/22 in December 1935. It handed over its aircraft to GB I/38 in September 1938 after having received MB 131s, which were themselves replaced during the Battle of France by Potez 63.11s. In the meantime the squadron had become GR II/22 like its partner I/22. This plane was part of the first series of Amiot 143s (up to N° 30) with a one-foot shorter fuselage and with differently shaped glazing.

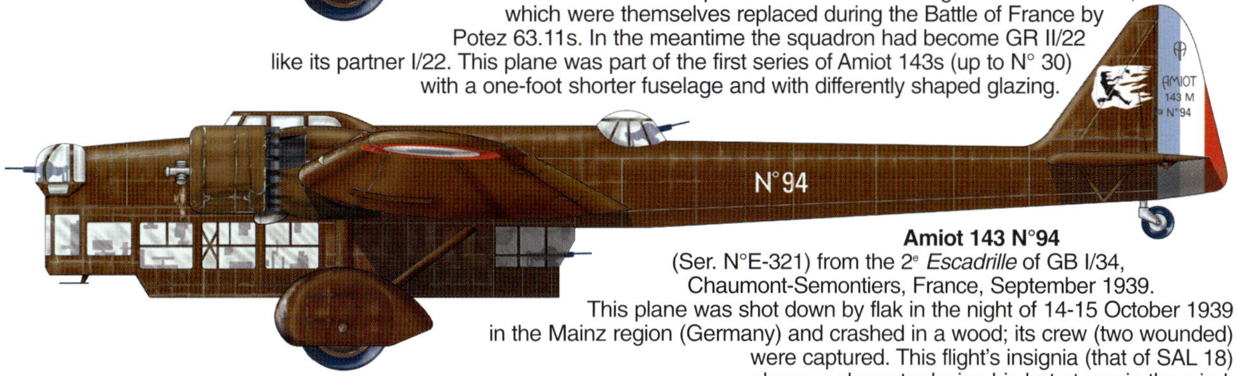

Amiot 143 N°94 (Ser. N°E-321) from the 2^{e} *Escadrille* of GB I/34, Chaumont-Semontiers, France, September 1939. This plane was shot down by flak in the night of 14-15 October 1939 in the Mainz region (Germany) and crashed in a wood; its crew (two wounded) were captured. This flight's insignia (that of SAL 18) shows a character losing his hat at sea in the wind, a drawing originally on a blue pennant.

Amiot 143

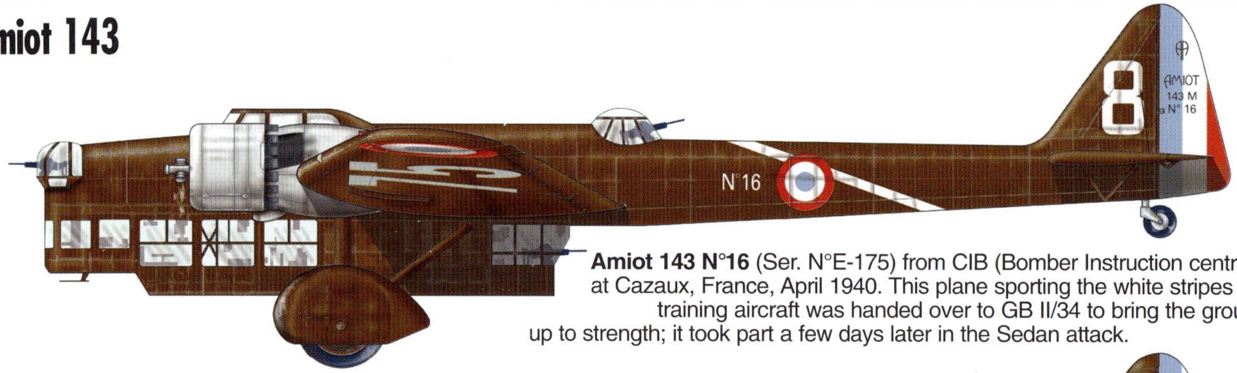

Amiot 143 N°16 (Ser. N°E-175) from CIB (Bomber Instruction centre) at Cazaux, France, April 1940. This plane sporting the white stripes of training aircraft was handed over to GB II/34 to bring the group up to strength; it took part a few days later in the Sedan attack.

Amiot 143 N°16 (Ser. N°E-175) from the 4e *Escadrille* of GB II/34, Troyes-Barberey, France, May 1940. This is the same plane as above but the upper surfaces have been camouflaged whereas the under sides have been painted black. The serial number has been covered over. In the middle of May 1940, *Groupement de Bombardement* N°9 (regrouping GBs I/34 and II/34) was still equipped with this type of bomber as its conversion to Amiot 351/354 was only partly completed.

Amiot 143 N°78 (Ser. N°E-301) from the 3e *Escadrille* of GB II/35, Pontarlier, France, December 1939. This squadron converted to Breguet 693, handed over its aircraft to GBs I/38 and II/38 in 1940 in order to make up their strength. Here again, these twin-engined planes were reserved for night missions and the lower surfaces have been repainted black which has covered the serial number on the underside.

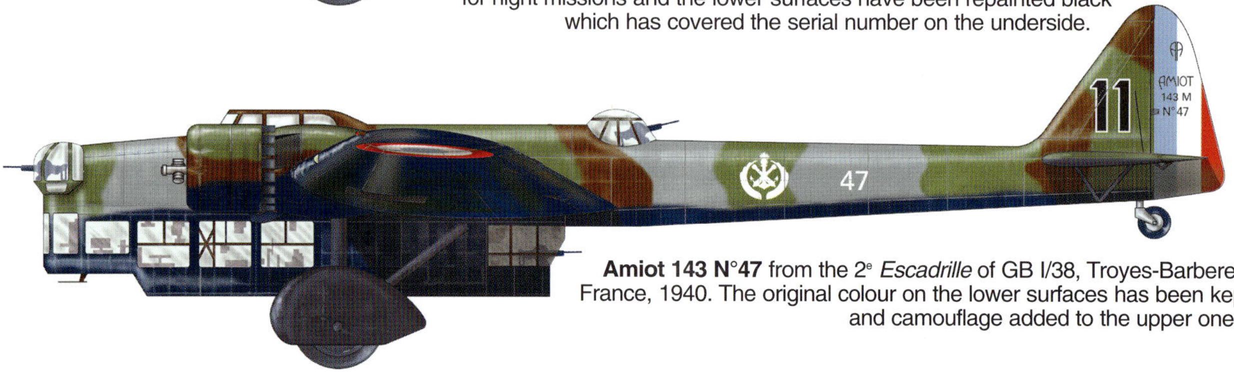

Amiot 143 N°47 from the 2e *Escadrille* of GB I/38, Troyes-Barberey, France, 1940. The original colour on the lower surfaces has been kept and camouflage added to the upper ones.

Amiot 143

Amiot 143 N° 106 (Ser. N°E-333) from the 2[e] *Escadrille* of GB I/38. Istres, France, September 1940. On this plane, completely painted black (or night blue?) with a white stripe around the fuselage roundel as imposed by the Armistice commissions, the wheel spats have been removed, a frequent practice on these bombers during operations, to prevent them clogging up with mud and seizing up.

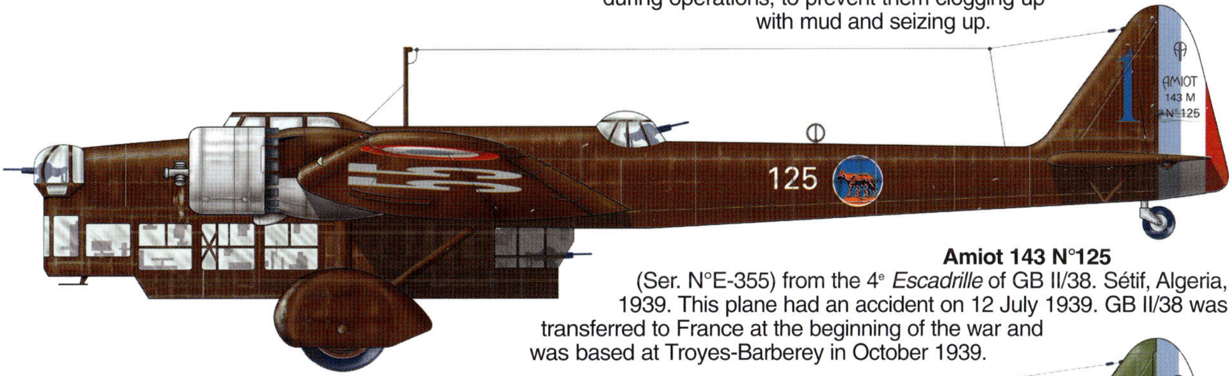

Amiot 143 N°125 (Ser. N°E-355) from the 4e *Escadrille* of GB II/38. Sétif, Algeria, 1939. This plane had an accident on 12 July 1939. GB II/38 was transferred to France at the beginning of the war and was based at Troyes-Barberey in October 1939.

Amiot 143 N°86 from the 4[e] *Escadrille* of GB II/38. Troyes-Barberey, France, May 1940. As its individual number painted on the tail shows, this was the 2nd Flight's commanding officer's plane. This was a unit which, after having missed its meet up with the fighters on 14 May 1940, turned round and did not therefore take part in the attacks on the bridges at Sedan. The *Groupement de Bombardement* N°10 (GB I and II/38) never received the modern bombers which had been planned to replace its Amiot 143s; its strength was even made up using MB 131s, in May 1940!

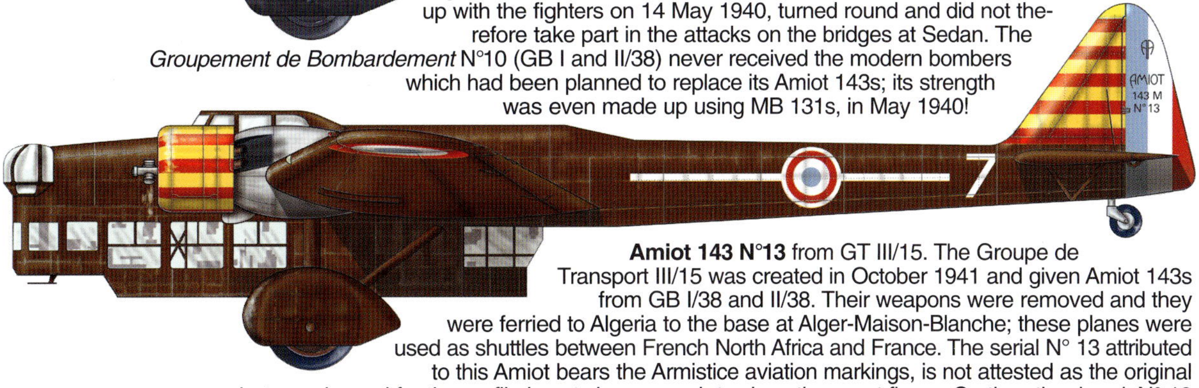

Amiot 143 N°13 from GT III/15. The Groupe de Transport III/15 was created in October 1941 and given Amiot 143s from GB I/38 and II/38. Their weapons were removed and they were ferried to Algeria to the base at Alger-Maison-Blanche; these planes were used as shuttles between French North Africa and France. The serial N° 13 attributed to this Amiot bears the Armistice aviation markings, is not attested as the original photograph used for the profile is not clear enough to show the exact figure. On the other hand, N° 13 did indeed operate within the group between 2 October and 27 December 1941.

Amiot 351 & 354

It was in 1936 at the XV Salon de l'Aéronautique, that Félix Amiot's SEMC unveiled its **Amiot 351**, a 'long-range mail carrier' derived from the 340BR3 (Bombardier de Représailles – Reprisal Bomber) and the 341B4 which dated back to the 1934 programme and whose military characteristics did not go unnoticed since it was fitted with a ventral bay with opening doors... The prototype, designated **Amiot 340 N°01** flew a little more than a year later at Istres on 6 December 1937, powered by two 920 bhp Gnôme-Rhône 14 N-0/1 engines. It was sent for trials to the CEMA at Villacoublay in March of the following year, after a which a series of modifications had to be carried out; before returning to the factory it did, however, fly General Vuillemin to Berlin in August on a 'disinformation' flight whose aim was to prove to the Germans that the French bombers of the period were indeed modern... After this bluff, in November the prototype was given new power plants, two Gnôme-Rhône 14 N-20/21s developing 1 020 bhp; a fourth crew member was added to operate the machine gun covering the lower rear sector, protection for the upper sector being ensured by a Hispano-Suiza 20-mm canon. Finally, a twin fin tail was fitted and this new version of the plane, designated the Amiot 351 N°01 started trials in January 1939.

As of 1938, the Amiot team had planned to bring out a series of machines derived from the 350, their power plants being the main difference between them. Apart from the Amiot 351 with Gnôme-Rhône engines, the others which were planned were;

– **Amiot 352** with Hispano-Suiza 12 Y-50/51 engines.

– **Amiot 353**, a variant fitted with two Rolls-Royce Merlin IIIs which in the end was never made.- Amiot 354 with Gnôme-Rhône 14 N-48/49 engines and a single tail fin.- Amiot 355, in fact production series aircraft N°12 fitted with Gnôme-Rhône 14 R-2/3 production series engines which were equipped with double two-stage compressors, and which was stored at Clermont-Ferrand because of the German advance.

– **Amiot 356** with Rolls-Royce Merlin X engines and also with a single tail fin; one example was built and was evacuated to Toulouse at the end of the Battle of France

– **Amiot 357** specialised in high altitude bombing with a pressurised cabin; the prototype was in the last stages of completion when the Germans arrived.

– finally the **Amiot 370**, a development of the original 'mail plane' designed solely for record breaking, particularly for the Paris- New York race which in the end was cancelled.

Above: **An Amiot 351 in the process of being finished at the Bourges factory. The front position has been covered with a tarpaulin and the aircraft has not yet been given its final camouflage.** *(Coll. J. Delmas)*

The official orders were placed in 1938. 130 of the 351, 353 and 354 versions were concerned by the order; these figures were considerably increased with the outbreak of war and reached 850 machines; Plan V even provided for monthly production to reach 150 machines. Even though when it made its first trials, the plane was ahead of its time and therefore absolutely suitable as a replacement for the old Amiot 143, under pressure form the Air Ministry, SEMC-Amiot had nonetheless to undertake a number of changes which, along with the strikes which studded the period, considerably delayed the start of production which had not really got under way even by the time France entered the war in September 1939.

The first production series aircraft was the Amiot 351 N°1 whose wings, compared with the original design had been shortened, the wing area reduced, the fuselage lengthened and the tail fins enlarged; the cockpit was redesigned and placed in the centre of the fuselage. Its first flight took place on 3 November 1939 at Orléans. The second aircraft of the production series was the Amiot 354 N°2, identical to the first save for the single tail unit (the tails of these aircraft were indeed interchangeable). The modifications which were deemed necessary after the first tests were carried out and this plane started its trials again in January 1940. The complicated arrangement used to assemble this twin-engined plane whose fuselage was built at Colombes (near Paris), the wings at Cherbourg (Normandy), the tail at Boulogne-Billancourt (Paris) and final assembly at le Bourget, partly explains why the production process was so long; to this relative disorganisation must be added official procrastination and other inevitable 'teething troubles' which always occur when a new machine is brought out. Thus only 21 machines were delivered to the Armée de l'Air by April 1940 instead of the original 285. One month later, this figure rose to 14 Amiot 351s and 40 Amiot 354s. Conversion had already started at unit level but a number of groups were obliged to use machines which were not '*bons de guerre*' (ready for war), since at the time only two groups had received this official qualification.

An experimental flight made up of personnel from units in the 21^{e} and 34^{e} *Escadres* (21th and 34th Wings) received this new model first; it was set up and received its first two bombers at the end

Opposite and bottom: **An Amiot 354 abandoned at Toulouse just after the Armistice. Note the wavy limit of the camouflage on the leading edges and the open front access hatch. The front machine gun is missing and perhaps was never fitted...** (Archives WingMasters)

of November 1939. By the following 10 May, GBs I/21 and II/21 were in the process of being converted and were to form *Groupement* 9 together with I/34 and II/34 which had each received... one machine. In the end, the conversion was never completed before the signature of the Armistice. Because of the lack of machines these units held on to their venerable Bloch 210s or Amiot 143s, GB I/34 for example, flying on to the very end on this type of machine and GB II/34 not even having had the opportunity to carry out real missions with its new aircraft... The situation got worse when the factories at Nangis and le Bourget were bombed which disorganised production even more.

The first war mission of the Amiot 351/354 occurred on 16 May 1940 when several machines carried out armed reconnaissance missions over Maastricht in Holland. A few days before the end of the fighting, the Air Ministry officially accepted about sixty Amiot 351/354s; this figure was slightly higher in reality as it is thought that between 80 and 85 aircraft were received unofficially. Thirteen of these machines were lost during their brief operational career (of which only three in combat), and the four squadrons which were equipped with them (GB I/21 and II/21, I/34 and II/34) were sent to French North Africa after 20 June so as to be able to attack Italy and Sardinia which had just entered the war against France from their new bases. So 37 machines crossed the Mediterranean but five did not reach their destination for various reasons. The remainder were too few to serve as a basis for the future of the operational groups, a situation which was not improved by the fact that the factories were now in the occupied part of France so the bombers were sent back from Meknes to Istres in France, where their groups were disbanded in August 1940.

Only five of them (three 354s, one 356 and one 370) were disarmed and used for long distance civil and paramilitary liaison after April 1941, some of them being seconded to Air France. At the end of 1942 when the Germans occupied the up-to-then 'Unoccupied Zone', they recovered four machines; it is known that one of these was used by the *Stab* (headquarters) of *Luftflotte* 3, and two by I./KG 200. It is worth noting that one machine which managed to escape capture in 1942 was put back into service at Dakar after being given new engines and was re-designated Amiot 358.

Thus ended the brief career of this elegant bomber which was much appreciated by its crews (especially following on their ancient Amiot 143s or Bloch 210s...), but its wings were clipped by France's dramatic circumstances before it was able to show its true mettle.

TECHNICAL SPECIFICATIONS

Type
Four-seat bomber

Motorisation
Two air-cooled 14-cylinder Gnôme-Rhône 14 N-48/49 radial engines developing 1 060 bhp at take-off and 1 100 bhp at 14,685 feet, and driving a 10 ft 11 in Ratier three-blade variable pitch propeller.

Dimensions
Height: 13 ft 9 in.
Wingspan: 75 ft 4 in.
Wing Area: 726.502 sq ft.
Unladen Weight: 14,300 lb.
Max. Weight: 24,860 lb.

Performances
Max. Speed: *256 mph at sea level; 303 mph at 16,500 ft.*
Cruising Speed: *262 mph*
Range: *1 543 miles with 1 760 lb of bombs and at 250 mph (2 187 miles at 220 mph).*
Max. Ceiling: *29 700 feet.*

Armement
One 120-round dorsal 20-mm HS 404 canon on an SAMM-AB 34 mount and two 7-mm MAC 34 machine guns, one on an SAMM-AB 20 mount in the nose and another firing from underneath (800 rounds). 1 760 lb of bombs (max. 2 750 lb) internally, normally four 440-lb bombs.

Amiot 351 & 354

Amiot 354 N°4 from GB II/21. La Ferté-Gaucher, France, May 1940. This plane was damaged on 28 May when it collided with another plane of the same type, N° 12, on the ground. When the GBs I/21, II/21 and I/34 received their first Amiots, they were not armed and so a makeshift machine gun was installed in the rear gunner's post, directly on the airfield.

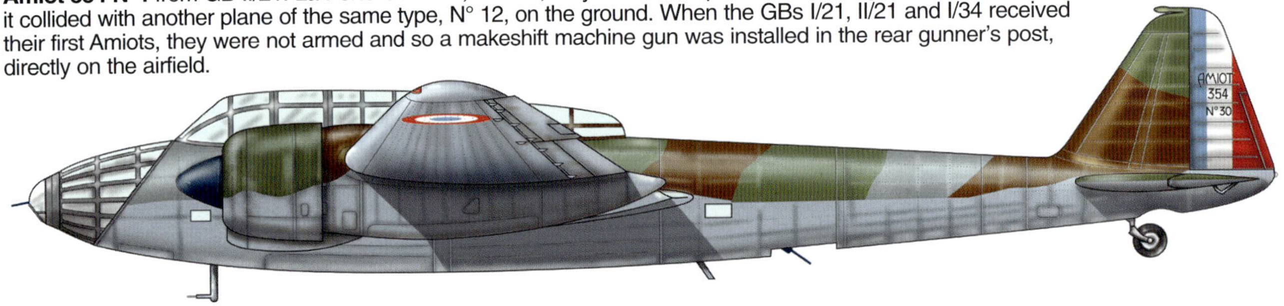

Amiot 354 N°30 from GB I/34. Montdidier, France, May 1940. This plane, one of the first to have been engaged in operational sorties was hit on 13 May 1940 by the flak over Maastricht as it was carrying out an armed reconnaissance mission. It had to make a forced landing in the countryside, it broke up and its pilot, Colonel François was wounded. It therefore had the sad privilege of being the first Amiot 354 shot down.

Amiot 354 N°31 from GB I/34. Bergerac, France, June 1940. The Amiot 351/354s had been sent into combat in great haste and urgency, and bore no unit insignia during the Battle of France; their serial number was put on the fuselage and served as the individual number as well. This plane was stored at Istres after the Armistice. At the time of the German offensive on 10 May 1940, GB I/34 was mostly equipped with old Amiot 143s; only three of the new, modern twin-engined planes were available. This Amiot was captured by the Germans in 1942.

Amiot 351 N°56. This plane which has been camouflage 'lizard' fashion and has the tricolour over the whole of the tail fin outer surfaces remains unique and was the 'first of the production series' Amiot 351. The first Amiot 351s which came off the production lines after 10 May 1940 were numbered from N° 56 onwards; none of the preceding aircraft (N°41 to 55), made by the SNCAC (ex-Farman), were completed when the German troops reached the factory. Tested at the CEMA, it was then assigned to GB II/34 just before it was transferred to French North Africa on 20 June. It returned to Istres to be stored there and was captured by the Germans when they invaded the Unoccupied Zone in November 1942. As can be seen, the rear defence Hispano-Suiza canon, just as effective as it was hard to handle, has been installed.

Amiot 351

Amiot 351 N°59 from GB II/21. Istres, France, beginning of 1941. The painting of compulsory markings set out by the Armistice Commissions (Official Note of 9 July 1940) changed only the decoration of these planes slightly; only the white stripe along the fuselage was interrupted to allow for the serial number, also painted white for easy visibility.

Amiot 351 N°73 from 4e *Escadrille* of GB II/21. Meknès, Morocco, July 1940. This plane bears the Armistice markings which were imposed during the summer of 1940. It has the flight insignia both on its fins and on the front of the fuselage.

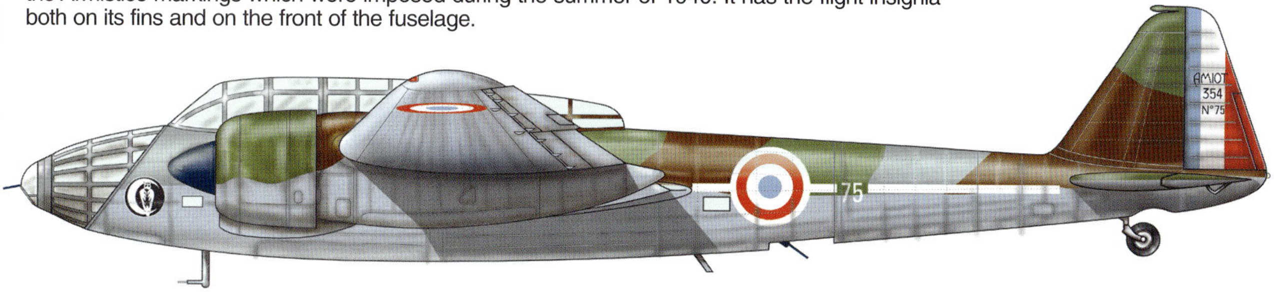

Amiot 351 N°75 from 4[e] *Escadrille* of GB II/21. Marseille-Marignane, France, 1941. This plane with the single tail fin of the Amiot 354 was converted so as to be used as a civilian liaison aircraft under the colours of the Air France Company and with the civil registration F-BAGS.

Amiot 351 N°81 from the 4e *Escadrille* of GB II/34. Meknès, Morocco, July 1940. This flight's insignia which took up the traditions of BR 224 shows a duck chasing a butterfly carrying an Iron Cross and wearing a spiked helmet. Most of the Amiot 351/354s which had crossed the Mediterranean at the end of June 1940 were ordered to return to France on the following 19 August. This transfer was carried out in two main formations several days later, only a handful of these twin-engined planes staying in French North Africa before being retired.

ANF-LES MUREAUX 113, 115 & 117

Above:
ANF-Les Mureaux 117 N°105 bearing a blazon resembling the insignia of flights of the 52^e^ *Escadre de Reconnaissance.*
(Archives WingMasters)

As was said in the introduction, French reconnaissance aviation was in a sorry state at the time of the declaration of war in September 1939. A good number of crews were mobilised on machines like the ANF-Les Mureaux 113 to 117 whose design went back ten years and whose replacement had been envisaged and even planned but never actually carried out.

The long and prolific line of ANF-Les Mureaux originated with the *Programme d'Avion R2* (for reconnaissance - two crew members) which was launched in 1928 in order to replace the Breguet 19 which was then in service, and which specified a two seater able to fly at 150 mph at a height of 16,500 feet, carrying a maximum bomb load of 5,500 lb over a distance of 560 miles. Nine tenders including in all seven prototypes were offered between 1929 and 1930 of which only three were finally retained; this included a Mureaux 110 and a 111, the first machines made by the new company which originated with the merger of the Ateliers des Mureaux and the Ateliers de Construction du Nord de la France (ANF). Both were single-engined, parasol monoplanes, made entirely of metal and designed by a team led by the engineer, André Brunet.

The first of the prototypes, the **ANF 110** N°01 flew in April 1931 whereas the second, N° 02 with a modified radiator, was used for fast ministerial transport. As for the **ANF 111**, it was officially presented at the 1930 Salon de l'Aéronautique. It was originally intended to be equipped with a Rolls-Royce supercharged engine but it was finally fitted with a Hispano-Suiza. In September 1931, ANF-Les Mureaux won the competition and a first official contract for ten ANF 110s was signed in 1932. This was changed in May 1933 to include two ANF 110s and eight ANF 112s and variants (ANF 113 and 114), all the planes having to be built at the les Mureaux factory in the Paris region. This modified contract was made up as follows: ANF 110 (N°1), ANF 111 (N°2), ANF112R2 (N°3 to 7), ANF112GR (N°8 '*Grand Raid*', an unarmed record plane) and finally ANF 114CN2 (N°9 and 10, two-seat night-fighters which were equipped in particular with searchlights and painted black and which had a rather short career). This machine was none other than the ANF 110-02 prototype, with a new turbo-charged Hispano-Suiza 12Y engine.

According to Plan I, the number of machines put into the line by France had to be reduced and those affected to reconnaissance dropped from 48.5% to 30% of the total. Whilst waiting for one machine capable of carrying out these three types of missions specified by the BCR programme (*Bombardement, Chasse et Rconnaissance* – bomber, fighter and reconnaissance) to be put into service, four flights had to be converted to ANF 113R2. With this in mind, an official contract was signed for 49 machines, spread over two ANF 113 ENTs (for *Entrainement* – training, and unarmed), two ANF 115R2s, forty-four ANF 113R2 and one ANF 117R2. These machines differed in the shape of the radiator and the load of fuel carried. The ANF 113 which flew for the first time on 15 March 1933 was none other than a Mureaux 112 fitted with a wooden two-blade propeller, replacing the Ratier three-blade metal propeller as an economy measure.

Displayed at the 1934 Salon de l'Aéronautique, the ANF 115R2 was in fact made up of an ANF 117R2 airframe fitted with larger tanks and equipped with a Hispano-Suiza 12Yers engine whose radiator was placed in the front and no longer in a ventral fairing as on the Mureaux 113 and 117, the aim of this being to improve cooling. The first machine flew on 6 March 1935 and very quickly demonstrated how superior it was to its stable mates. In all, including pre-series machines, 122 Mureaux 115 came off the production lines, an amendment to the June 1935 contract changing 30 ANF 115R2B2 (N°1 to 30) into 'mini BCRs' since they could be armed with a Hispano-Suiza canon above the engine, firing through the propeller arc and could, if needs be, be used as… fighters!

Finally the ANF 117 was identical to the ANF 113 but had reinforced strutting and the same fuel tanks as the 115, which increased its range from 575 to 937 miles. 119 examples were built and the first machine of the series (ANF 113 N°11) was delivered to the Armée de l'Air on 13 June 1934 and the last at the end of the following February. The ANF 115s were delivered in July 1934.

Trials carried out on the ANF 112 had shown that the machine could stand an increased load without this affecting its performances in any great way so an amendment dated 23 February 1934 increased the original order to 17 ANF 117s (N°60 to 76) which were

ANF-Les Mureaux 115 N°1 photographed as it came out of the factory. *(DR)*

delivered between January and May 1935; the airframe of the last machine was used to built the ANF 115.The Mureaux 113 started to replace the Potez 25 in Metropolitan France and went into service from January 1935, GR (*Groupes de reconnaissance* – Reconnaissance squadrons) I/54 and I/55 receiving their ANF 117 R2s in the following March.

The retirement of the Breguet 19 night fighter meant that three squadrons equipped with this type had to be urgently converted, so 40 Mureaux 113 were converted into two-seat night fighters (CN2) after being fitted with a higher rear turret, a modification which was also made on certain 'normal' Mureaux 113s and 117s. The transfer of the equipment originally meant for the reconnaissance units was made up for with an extra order for 40 Mureaux 117, whilst in the autumn of 1935, 30 of the 40 Mureaux 113CN2s were transferred to GCN (*Groupe de Chasse de Nuit*–night fighter squadron) II/41 and *Escadrille* 3/42.

In April 1935, within the context of the '1 500 aircraft Plan', specified for by Plan I, a further 60 ANF 117 were ordered in addition to those already ordered to replace the night fighter conversions. As they were also intended to support the planes in the BCR Programme, they were designated ANF117 R2B2, the role of bomber being made possible by the addition of underwing bomb-launchers enabling 880-lb bomb loads to be carried. Deliveries of these machines went on until April 1936, the production lines for the ANF 117 being finally wound up in July of the following year.

On the eve of the Second World War, the Armée de l'Air had 221 Mureaux: 28 ANF 113s, 100 ANF 115s and 97 ANF 117s. Out of 36 GAO (*Groupes Aériens d'Observation* – air observation squadrons) based in Metropolitan France, nine were equipped with Mureaux 115s and an equivalent number of ANF 117s, unit strength being made up with Potez 25s. It was also this plane which had the sad honour to be the first French plane shot down during WWII; this was a Mureaux 115 of GAO 553 on 8 September 1939, eight other machines being lost during the same month. Faced with severe losses right from the first weeks of the conflict – in all 171 out of the 228 machines in service were lost during the Phoney War and the Battle of France – the authorities started by restricting flying time for observation flights to fifteen minutes, before limiting the use of the Mureaux even further before the conversion of the crews and the arrival of the new replacement Potez 63.11.150 Mureaux were still in the line at the end of October 1939 and there was still a large number of them at the start of the German onslaught on 10 May 1940, since there were still about a hundred left in the groups and the test centres; their presence was explained by the fact that at the time they had still not been replaced and were therefore still operational, alongside the Breguet 270s and Potez 390s.

Because of their great vulnerability however, the Mureaux were only rarely used during the Battle of France and the 53 survivors (five ANF 113s, 36 ANF 115s and 12 ANF 112s) at the time of the Armistice were all scrapped, including two ANF 115s of GAO 1/50 which had managed to reach North Africa under their own steam.

Below:

ANF-Les Mureaux 117 from GAO I/551 was entirely camouflaged and was damaged during an air raid, on 10 May 1940. *(BA)*

TECHNICAL SPECIFICATIONS

Type
Two-seat Observation aircraft.

Power plant
One Hispano-Suiza 12Ydrs (113 and 117) or 12Ycrs (115) rated at 650 bhp (113) or 860 bhp (115 and 117), driving an 11 ft 6 in three-blade propeller.

Dimensions
Length: 33 ft 1 in (113), 33 ft 6 in (117) and 50 ft 10 in (115).
Height: 11 ft 4 in.
Wingspan: 50 ft 10 in.
Wing Area: 375.628 sq ft.
Unladen Weight: 3,564 lb (113), 3,863 lb (115).
Max. Weight: 5,649 lb (113), 5,922 lb (115)

Performance
Max. Speed: 170 mph (113), 171 mph (117) and 167 mph (115).
Max. Range: 562 miles (113 and 117), 937 miles (115).

Armament
2 Vickers cowling-mounted machine guns; 2 Lewis guns in the rear turret and one firing through the floor fired with the foot (113 and 117). One MAC 34 firing through the propeller arc or 2 cowling mounted Vickers machine guns; 2 turret mounted Lewis guns or one MAC 34 on a flexible mount; one Lewis gun firing through the floor and fired with the foot (115). Some ANF 117s could carry 880 lb of bombs on underwing pylons.

ANF-Les Mureaux 115 & 117

ANF-Les Mureaux 117 N°73
(Ser. N° X-071) from GAO 515. Connantre, France, September 1940. This plane, still equipped with its wheel spats, bears the original livery given to all the Mureaux: dark '*tableau*' green on all the surfaces, except for the engine cowling which was left bare. The insignia was painted on the fuselage and was replaced, in the same place at the beginning of 1940, by a roundel.

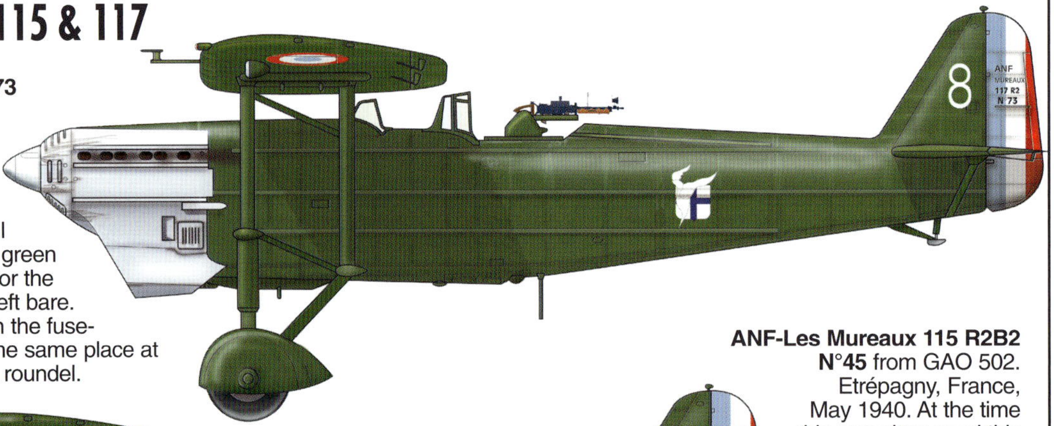

ANF-Les Mureaux 115 R2B2 N°45 from GAO 502. Etrépagny, France, May 1940. At the time this squadron used this type of machine alongside the Potez 63.11s which were clearly more modern. Camouflage has been reduced to its most simple form since only the engine cowling has been painted over with brown patches, to make it less visible.

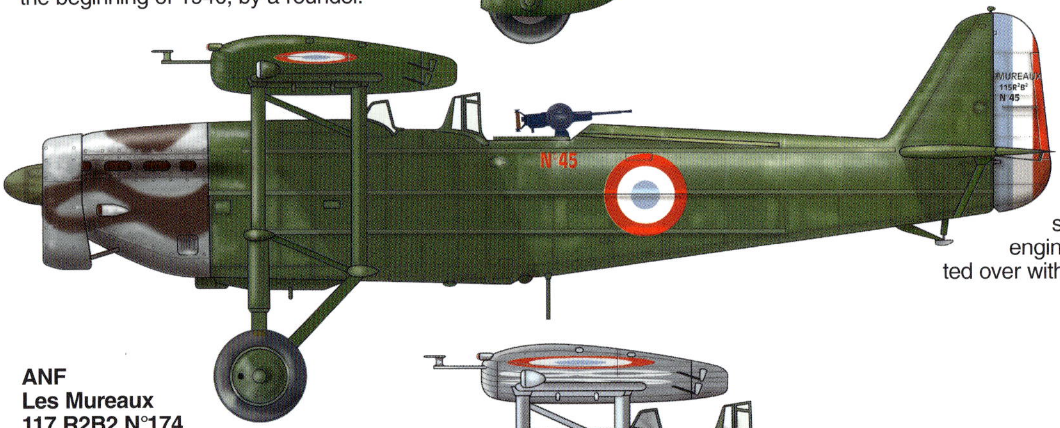

ANF Les Mureaux 117 R2B2 N°174
(Ser. N° X-398) from GAO I/551. Attigny, France, September 1939.
This plane, damaged on 8 August 1939 at la Malmaison (Aisne) bears the camouflage applied to the Mureaux after the Munich crisis, the original green being kept on the upper surfaces and the lower ones painted light grey-blue; the serial number was repainted black.

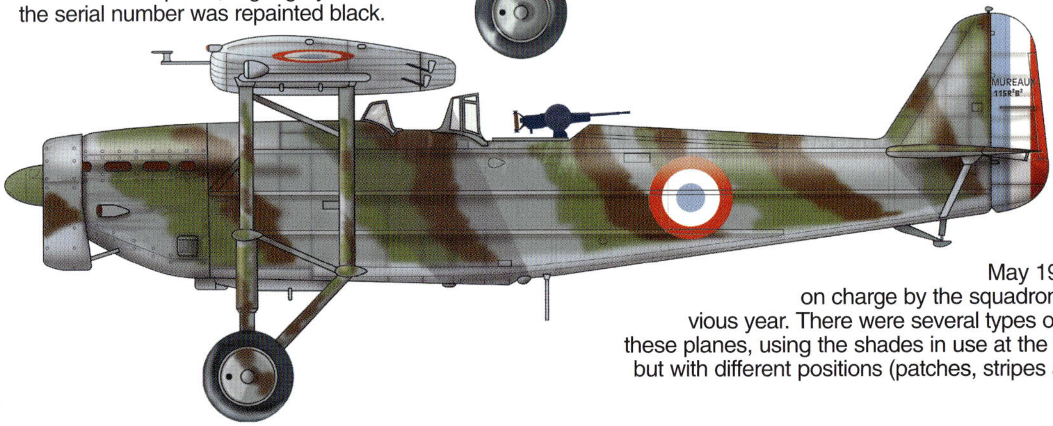

ANF-Les Mureaux 115 R2B2 N°119
(Ser. N° X-690) from GAO I/520. Morhange, France, May 1940. This plane was taken on charge by the squadron in September of the previous year. There were several types of camouflage schemes on these planes, using the shades in use at the time in the Armée de l'Air, but with different positions (patches, stripes and as here, lattice work).

ANF-Les Mureaux 115 & 117

ANF-Les Mureaux 115 R2B2 N°21 (Ser. N° X-420) from GAO 507. Thales, France, September 1939. Nicknamed '*la Glandouille*' ('lazy bones'), this plane had to make a forced landing on 20 September 1939 after having been attacked by several Me 109s near Saralbe in the Moselle. The camouflage has hidden the unit insignia, and the serial number on the underside of the wings has been repainted black.

ANF-Les Mureaux 115 R2B2 N°107 (Ser. N° X-678) from GAO I/520. Delme-Morhange, France, September 1939. This plane, escorted by five Morane 406s was damaged by German fighters on 24 September 1939 whilst on a photographic reconnaissance mission. The pilot, *Sous-Lieutenant* Petit managed to reach his airfield aboard his very much damaged plane with his severely wounded observer, *Lieutenant* Bernard.

ANF-Les Mureaux 117 R2B2 N°121 from GAO I/551. Etain, France, May 1940. The Mureaux which were still operational at the time of the Battle of France (in this GAO, alongside the Potez 63.11s which should have replaced all of them…) were very elaborately camouflaged so as to make them the least vulnerable as possible, the serial number being repainted in red under the rear cockpit.

ANF-Les Mureaux 115 R2B2 (Number and Serial Number unknown) used for training by the EAA at Salon-de-Provence in the spring of 1941. It was one of the rare planes of this type to remain in service long enough to wear the Armistice air force markings.

Arsenal VG 33 – 39

In the context of the 1937 programme whose aim was to replace the MS 406 which at the time had just started its flight testing, four machines took part in the official competition: the Dewoitine D.520, the CAO 200, the Morane-Saulnier 450 and the Arsenal VG 33. The latter was the result of studies made during the thirties on producing aircraft from non-strategic materials (mainly wood which needed less qualified labour for production) whose performances were nevertheless comparable with aircraft made of metal, which were more expensive and more difficult to build.

The Arsenal de l'Aéronautique Company, which was created especially to experiment with these new techniques had been given the project and two of its engineers, Michel Vernisse and Jean Galtier (hence the VG of the designation) worked on the concept of a fighter with two engines installed in tandem, the VG 20. From this developed the VG 30, designed to rival with the Caudron 713, and presented at the 1936 Salon de l'Aéronautique. This plane was originally to have been powered by a 610 bhp Potez 12Dc engine, but this was not available at the time, so finally a 690 bhp Hispano-Suiza 12 Xcrs was used. The prototype's first flight took place on 6 October 1938, an official order for 200 machines having been made several weeks earlier following on the Munich crisis. At the time the VG 30 was considered as a flying test bed foreshadowing a potential, more powerful production series aircraft and its performances although better than those of the Morane 406 with its more powerful engine were nonetheless considered on the whole to be disappointing.

Very early on, a whole line of fighters was planned differing mainly

Above, below and opposite page, top: **Arsenal VG 33 N°7 seen at Toulouse-Blagnac where it fell back at the end of June 1940 after having been part of GC I/55 at Bordeaux. Note that the camouflage on the engine cowling is different from the rest of the fuselage and that the undercarriage does not have its doors.**
(Archives WingMasters)

in the engines fitted which gave rise to a series of variants because of the different installation of various items of equipment in the airframe (radiators, etc). All these machines were made however of wood and mounted plywood (i.e. covered with varnished canvas and painted), except for the engine cowling which was naturally made of metal.

The **VG 31** was thus very logically the first planned development. Compared with the VG 30, it was to have had a Hispano-Suiza 12 Y-31 and a reduced wing area. It was finally never assembled but as will be seen later, its fuselage was used to make VG 33 N°3.

The fate of **VG 32** was scarcely more enviable. It appeared after the VG 33 because of delays in delivering its American power plant, an Alison V-1710 C-15 and it never flew because German troops arrived. On the other hand the **VG 33** managed to reach the production series stage even though this was, as before with other planes, curtailed for military reasons. It was powered by a Hispano-Suiza 12 Y-31 developing 860 bhp; N°01 took off for the first time at the end of the spring of 1938 and started official trials from the following August. On this occasion it reached a maximum speed of 344 mph at 17 160 feet, which meant it was faster than its rival, the Dewoitine D.520 which was made with strategic materials, and this was in spite of the fact that it had a less powerful engine.

VG 33 N°2 was to have received an even more powerful Hispano-Suiza 12 Y-45 reaching 910 bhp. In fact this machine, although it was built, was never actually assembled. Its wings were matched to the fuselage of the VG 31, the whole ending up as VG 33 N°3, whereas its fuselage went into making the **VG 34**. This was equipped with the engine originally intended for VG 33 N°2 which finally flew in the spring of 1940 and reached a speed of 360 mph.

The **VG 35** remained at the project stage. This version was to have been fitted with a 1 100 bhp Hispano-Suiza 12 Y-51 engine which was finally installed in the **VG 36** whose silhouette had to be modified to take it (a smaller ventral radiator and a higher rear section of the fuselage). This machine was only able to carry out a limited number of trial flights. Two further projects were planned: the

VG 37 with 1 000 bhp Hispano-Suiza and the **VG 38** powered by a Hispano-Suiza 77 with two Brown-Boveri exhaust-driven turbo-superchargers.

The **VG 39** was the last variant of this prolific line. Equipped with the most powerful engine ever fitted into an aircraft of the VG 30 series, the 1 280 bhp Hispano-Suiza 89ter, it was armed with six 7.5 mm machine guns. After reaching the very promising speed of 393 mph it was finally conveyed to Toulouse-Blagnac at the time of the German advance in the spring of 1940. It was supposed to give rise to a production series machine, the VG 39bis with the same fuselage as the VG 36 (smaller radiator) and finally a Hispano 12Z. The French engine makers were unable to keep up a sufficiently sustained production rhythm, so it was decided to call upon other makers, particularly Americans.

This is why a second series version was planned, equipped with an Alison motor, also to be installed in the fuselage of a VG 36 but with the wings of a VG 39, the extra weapons they contained being intended to replace the canon firing through the propeller boss which could not be fitted into the fuselage at the same time as the American engine. An official order for 220 machines was made on 12 September 1939, deliveries of the machine to be made between January and April 1940 with a further 500 machines being required. Unfortunately, these plans were never realised since in April 1940, only one machine had been received by the Armée de l'Air and sent for trials to Cazaux. Seven machines which were considered 'ready for war' since they were practically complete were received by EAA 301 in June and July 1940, the machines available being regrouped on 10 June at Villacoublay because the unit to which they were supposed to be delivered, the GC I/2, could not under the circumstances, receive them. It was the Etampes patrol which was ordered to ferry the aircraft to Bordeaux, the remaining examples were to put out of action before the French troops fell back. Two of these machines, the prototype (01) and N°7 were assigned to GC I/55, an ephemeral unit gathering together various types of fighters and whose operational life, begun on 18 June, only lasted one week during which several combat missions were nevertheless carried out; Arsenal N°7 finally fell back on Blagnac where it joined some other Arsenals which had arrived there under their own steam.

It is estimated that when hostilities ceased about 160 airframes were in the process of being made of which forty or so were almost finished. On the other hand, the number of Arsenals which actually came out of the factory is still rather hard to evaluate (ten planes actually operational and several others in flying condition but nevertheless incomplete). Five series machines to which VG 33 N°1 must be added were in any case recovered by the Germans after the June 1940 Armistice.

Below: **the prototype of the Arsenal VG 33 (N°01) seen during trials at Villacoublay. Compared with the production series machines, the Pitot tube and the windshield (fitted with a small pane at its base) were different whereas the undercarriage was made by Messier, replaced later by an Olaer.** *(SHAA)*

TECHNICAL SPECIFICATIONS (VG 33)

Type
Single seat fighter.

Power plant:
One 860 bhp 12 cylinder Hispano-Suiza liquid-cooled inline engine driving a 12 ft 4 in diameter three blade Chauvière propeller.

Dimensions
***Length:** 28 ft 2 in.*
***Height:** 11 ft.*
***Wingspan:** 35 ft 7 in.*
***Wing Area:** 148.529 sq ft.*
***Unladen Weight:** 4 510 lb.*
***Max. Weight:** 6 371 lb.*

Performance
***Max. Speed:** 348 mph at 17 160 ft.*
***Max. Range:** 750 miles.*
***Practical ceiling:** 36,000 ft.*

Armament
One 60-round 20-mm Hispano-Suiza HS 404 canon firing through the engine. Four MAC 1934 M39 machine guns with 500 rounds each.

Arsenal VG 33 to VG 39

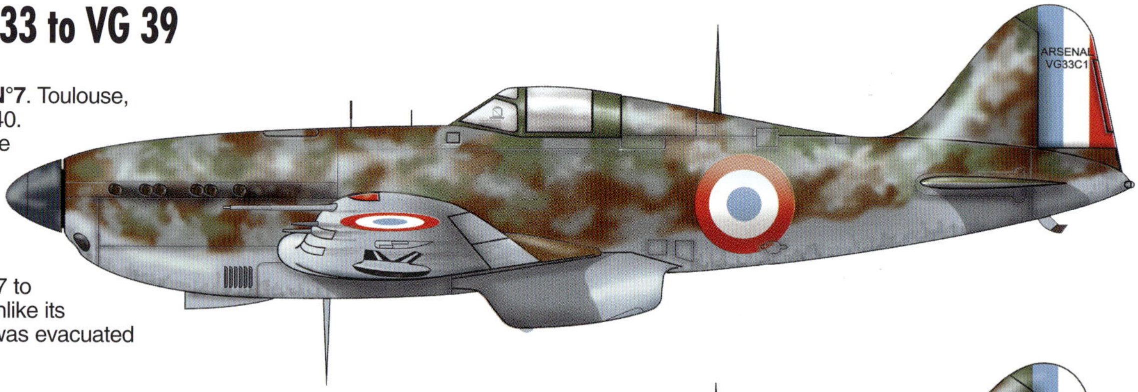

Arsenal VG 33 N°7. Toulouse, France, June 1940. With the prototype N°01, this VG 33 was part of the short-lived GC I/55, operational at Bordeaux from 17 to 24 June 1940. Unlike its running-mate, it was evacuated to Toulouse.

Arsenal VG 33 N°6. Ferried from Villacoublay to Clermont-Ferrand by one of the pilots of the *Patrouille d'Etampes* created in May 1940, this plane was to be used as a production model in the Michelin factory which according to the original plans had been entrusted with part of the construction of this machine. The war decided otherwise…

Arsenal VG 36 N°01. The VG 36 of which a single prototype (N°01) was built, was the definitive variant of the VG 35 which used the same engine (Hispano-Suiza 12 Y-51) and should have replaced the VG 33 on the assembly lines in the middle of production. Having flown for the first time on 14 May 1940, this prototype was finally destroyed at La Roche-sur-Yon where it had been evacuated.

Arsenal VG 39 N°01. Only the prototype of this promising version was completed and flew on 3 May 1940 before being sent to Toulouse where it too was destroyed. The longer and more slender engine cowling had had to be fitted because of the installation of the powerful Hispano-Suiza 12 Z engine rated at 1 200 bhp which was longer than its predecessors.

Blériot-Spad 510

Above:
Blériot-SPAD 510 N°14 from the 3e *Escadrille* of GC II/7. This unit was re-equipped with the MS 406 just before mobilisation, in the summer of 1939. This plane is made entirely of aluminium with the upper surfaces camouflaged with khaki. *(Coll. J. Delmas)*

If one takes into account the whole of its career one has to admit that the Blériot-SPAD's only claim to fame was to have been the last biplane fighter ordered and used by the Armée de l'Air. Designed within the framework of the 1930 C1 Programme by the engineer, André Herbemont, it was in competition with the Dewoitine 500 and the Loire 43. One example was officially ordered from the Blériot-SPAD Company (the famous 'Société de Production des Avions Deperdussin' of the Great War which since then had become the 'Société Anonyme pour l'Aviation et ses Dérivés') at the end of 1931 to be tried out. It was a biplane with an all metal fuselage and whose rear section was of monocoque construction made of Duralumin; the wings and tail were made of canvas. It was powered by a liquid-cooled Vee-12 Hispano-Suiza engine which turned out not to have a very good performance which was a crippling failing affecting the majority of French machines during the pre-war period.

The prototype's first flight took place on 6 January 1933 and the plane underwent a number of different tests during which the fuselage was lengthened by 16 inches to reduce problems of instability which had been come to light; the tail surface was increased to improve directional stability. The first and last official order was placed in August 1935; the sixty machines ordered started arriving at the beginning of the following year. In this lot the last two machines were fitted with the Hispano-Suiza 12 Xcrs which enabled a 20-mm canon to be installed between the two rows of cylinders and fire through the propeller hub.

The 7e *Escadre de chasse* (Fighter Wing) was the only unit to use this type, the SPAD 510 being assigned to the GC I/7 in May 1937 and to the GC II/7 in the following July. This aircraft was intended to ensure the transition between the Morane 225 and the MS 405/406 for which everybody was waiting. One can imagine the pilots' disappointment when they received the same type of aircraft which hardly performed better than the old biplanes they were supposed to replace. The inevitable teething troubles (especially a weak undercarriage) were finally solved and the machines were finally declared 'fit for war' only in February 1938, once radio had been installed on board. Their only feat of arms during their brief time in the group was to have taken part in the 'Weiser Circus' alongside the Morane 225s. This was an acrobatic patrol whose speciality was to present its machines in flight, joined together with ropes to which pennants were attached. On this occasion, the SPAD 510 showed off its great manoeuvrability which could not however make up for its weak performances. The planned arrival of the MS 405/406 having been speeded up by the invasion of Czechoslovakia in 1938, the Spads were gradually retired from front line service and sent to the depots. In fact, while GC I/7 no longer had any these aircraft in February 1938, GC II/7 had barely finished converting when war started the following September.

Now they were available, ten or so Blériot-Spad 510s were sent to French North Africa where they served in several ERCs (*Escadrilles Régionales de Chasse* –regional fighter flights) which were units specially created in the thirties to ensure that reserve pilots were trained up. In May 1940 a fighter group, GC III/5 was even formed with the units which were still available (ERC 572 and 574) but their age only allowed them to carry out training flights.

In Metropolitan France, the planes which were still in the depots when war started were got back into service in ERC 3/561 and 4/561 which then were mobilised like all the reserve units as of 24 August 1939. Based at St Inglevert (Pas de Calais) and Villacoublay, and also using some just as venerable NiD 622s, these flights formed the GARC (*Groupe Aérien Régional de Chasse*) II/561 which moved into Havre-Octeville. This unit started converting onto Bloch 151 in the following December and became a real fighting unit, GC III/10, on 18 January 1940 and gradually replaced its Blériot-Spad 510s which dwindled in number as the weeks went by and which were relegated to training duties. The last biplane in the Armée de l'Air thus ended a career which had not exactly been very brilliant, without facing the enemy, which most likely enabled it to avoid a worse fate...

TECHNICAL SPECIFICATIONS

Type
Single-seat fighter
Power plant
One V-12 water-cooled Hispano-Suiza 12 Xbrs engine developing 690 bhp at 13,200 feet.
Dimensions
Length: *24 ft 7 in.*
Height: *12 ft 3 in.*
Wingspan: *29 ft 2 in.*
Wing Area: *236.786 sq ft.*
Unladen Weight: *2,750 lb.*
Max. Weight: *4,026 lb.*
Performance
Max. Speed: *202.5 mph at 3 300 feet, 231 mph at 16,500 feet.*
Max. Range: *546 miles.*
Practical Ceiling: *34,650 ft.*
Armament
Four 7.5-mm MAC 1934 machine guns under the wings.

Blériot-Spad 510

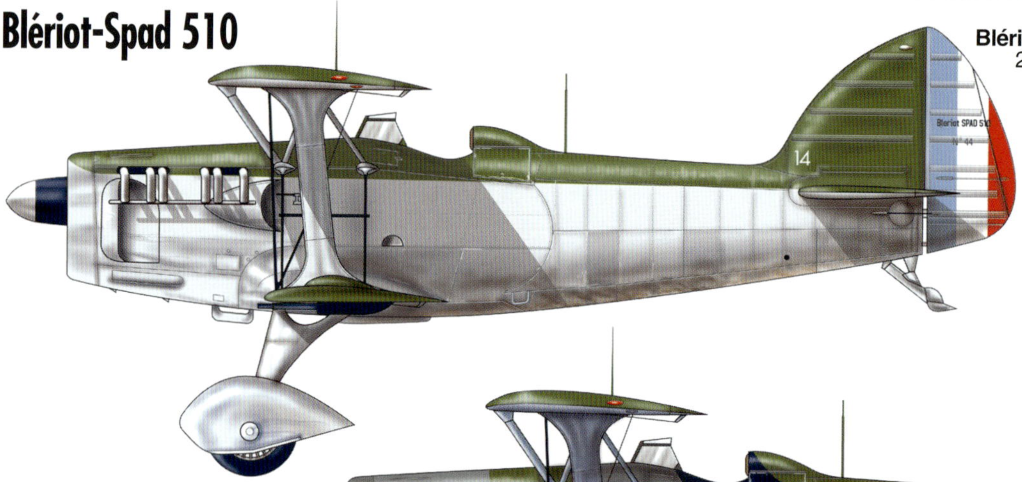

Blériot-SPAD 510 N°44 from the 2e *Escadrille* of GARC II/561. Le Havre-Octeville, France, November 1939. This *Groupe Aérien Regional de Chasse* (Regional air fighter squadron) was formed in October 1939 with ERCs 3/561 and 4/561 (reserve flights) and was the only one equipped with this plane, the Armée de l'Air's last biplane, based in Metropolitan France.

Blériot-SPAD 510 N°12 from the 2e *Escadrille* of GC III/5. Bir Guenich, Tunisia, end of June 1940. When the 7e Escadre de Chasse, the only user of the SPAD 510, finally received its MS 406s, ten or so of its former fighters were sent to North Africa where they served in the ERCs before being assigned to GC III/5, which in the end only used them for training because they were so out-of-date.

Blériot-SPAD 510 N°56 from CIC (*Centre d'Instruction à la Chasse* – Fighter training centre). Montpellier, France, end of June 1940. This plane bears the camouflage applied originally on all SPAD 510s: the plane was painted entirely aluminium with the khaki upper surfaces.

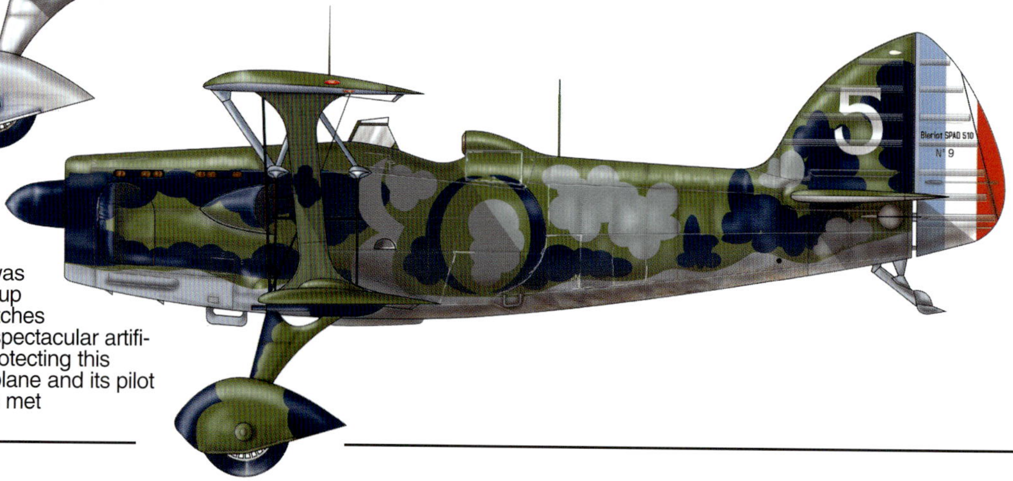

Blériot-SPAD 510 N°9 from ERC III/561. Le Havre-Octeville, France, October 1939. Piloted by *Sergent-Chef* Sigeot, this biplane bears one of the most extraordinary camouflage schemes in the Armée de l'Air of the time. It was painted in the field and made up of rounded grey and black patches on a khaki background. This spectacular artifice was not very effective in protecting this out-of-date machine and the plane and its pilot were very lucky never to have met the enemy…

Bloch MB 131

In the context of the BCR (*Bombardement, Chasse, Renseignement* – Bomber, Fighter, Reconnaissance) program, an official request was launched in August 1933 for an aircraft able to carry one ton of bombs over a maximum distance of 800 miles at 220 mph at a height of 13 200 ft. Eight manufacturers replied among which the SEMC-Amiot (144), Breguet (460), Farman (420), Potez (541) and the Société Aéronautique Bordelaise (SAB 60). Couzinet (190) and Dewoitine (420) only submitted simple projects. Bloch proposed its **MB 130** which took up the basic concept of the MB 210, i.e. an all-metal low-wing aircraft; the prototype took off in June 1934 with fixed undercarriage at first.

As these trials entailed certain modifications, an order for 40 machines was placed a year later in October 1935, when the BCR concept was being called into question because it seemed so totally unsuited to its intended missions. Bloch had already considered designing another aircraft derived from his first machine but it was now more specialised. He proposed his MB 131RB4 (Reconnaissance and Bombing with 4 crew members) and the original order, at first suspended, was replaced by a second in April 1936 for the same number of machines, but this time for the new model whose prototype first flew on the following 12 August.

TECHNICAL SPECIFICATIONS

Type
Four-seat bomber and reconnaissance aircraft.

Power plants
Two 14 cylinder air-cooled Gnôme-Rhône 14N-10/11 radial engines developing 950 bhp at 12 000 feet.

Dimensions
Length: *58 ft 9 in.*
Height: *13 ft 6 in.*
Wingspan: *67 ft.*
Wing Area: *560.752 sq ft.*
Unladen Weight: *10,307 lb.*
Weight Laden: *17,380 lb.*
Max. Take-off Weight: *18,898 lb.*

Performances
Max. Speed: *188.75 mph at sea level, 218 mph at 12,210 feet.*
Cruising speed: *168.75 mph at 12,210 feet.*
Range: *625 miles – 812 miles maximum.*
Practical Ceiling: *23,652 feet.*

Armament
One 500-round MAC 34 machine gun mounted in the nose, another in the dorsal turret (1,500 rounds) and one in the ventral gondola (1,500 rounds), 1,760 lb maximum of bombs in various combinations.

Above:
Bloch MB 131 N° 109 from the 2e Escadrille of GR I/14 (two-colour stripe on the fuselage) warming up its engines. Note the wavy limit between the upper (Khaki) and the lower (light grey-blue) colours which was typical of these two-engined planes.
(Coll. J. Delmas)

In the following November on the occasion of the *Salon de l'Aéronautique*, a second prototype was unveiled which differed from its predecessor in some important ways: a fifth crew member was added, the dorsal turret moved forward, another ventral one introduced and the tailplane bracing struts removed. This machine flew for the first time on 5 May 1937.

Some vibration problems appeared during the trials and the horizontal tail surface was reduced and positive dihedral was introduced. The first production series aircraft (MB 131 N°1) once modified flew a short while after the second prototype in May 1937, the production series using Gnôme-Rhône 14 N-10/11 engines which were just as powerful as the GR 14K Mistral Major of the prototypes but better cooled. Various armament tests were also carried out, for example a 20-mm canon being installed in the forward glazed nose, replaced afterwards by a single 7.5-mm machine gun. The initial semi-retractable gondola was replaced by a fixed position armed with a defensive rearward-firing machine gun.

A first batch of 14 machines was only equipped for reconnaissance (**MB 131R4**), followed by five training planes (**MB 131 Ins** – for instruction), the 19th production series machine (N°21) being the first 'real' **MB131RB4**. A further 100 machines were then delivered, the last of which (N°122) being accepted by GR I/36 in October 1939. From the outside nothing distinguished the RB4 from an R4 except for the wheels of the RB4's main undercarriage which were larger and the bomb bay which was fitted with different Alkan bomb launchers.

Above:
MB 131s lined up at Toulouse just after the June 1940 Armistice. Some of these planes continued to serve with the Vichy Air Force after being converted to target tugs.
(Archives WingMasters)

This machine did not give rise to any variants except for the **MB 133** which flew for the first time on 1 October 1937 and which was nothing other than an MB 131 fitted with a twin-tail and powered by Hispano-Suiza 14AA engines; and the **MB 134B4** whose three prototypes were ordered in March 1938. Only one was built and flew in July 1939. It was damaged beyond repair on landing on 21 April of the following year. This plane was not produced in series, the Leo 451 being chosen in its stead.

The 22e *Escadre* was the first unit to receive the new plane from June 1938 onwards followed by GR I/55 in January 1939, the 14th GAA (*Groupement Aérien Autonome*) and GR I/35 the following spring. On 3 September 1939 when hostilities started, the MB 131 was used by the 14th GAA, GR I/22 and II/22, I/55 and II/55 in France itself and by GR I/61 in North Africa.

The first missions carried out by 14th GAA and GR II/22 and II/55 aircraft very quickly showed the MB 131 to be out of date; it was decided to use it only for night missions and to speed up the conversion of its pilots onto Potez 63.11. Some machines were transferred to GR I/36 and II/36 at the time still equipped with Potez 540s or 637 while waiting for future conversion. Thus on 10 May when the Germans launched their offensive, only GR I/61 based in French North Africa was still equipped with this twin-engined plane. After the Armistice, a certain number of surviving examples were converted to target tugs, the ventral gondola being modified to take the cable and winch system. That was the end of the story of twin-engined plane which was already out of date when put into service and which was never able to accomplish the missions for which it had been originally designed.

Opposite:
The cockpit of an MB 131 seen from the fuselage walkway, on the right of the bomb bay. The bombardier's well-glazed position can be seen in the front.
(Archives WingMasters)

Bloch MB 131

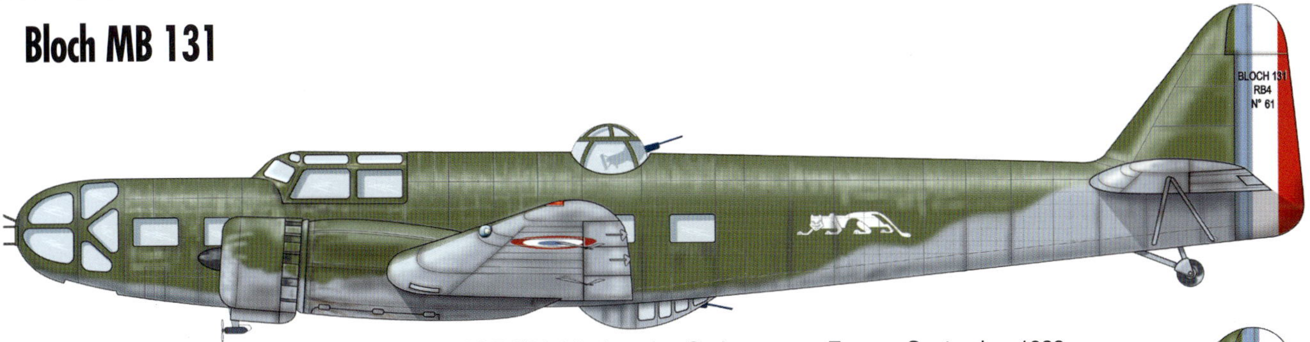

Bloch MB 131 N°31 from the 1re *Escadrille* of GR I/14. Martigny-les-Gerbonveaux, France, September 1939. Running out of fuel while returning from a mission during the night of 20 September, this plane made a belly landing near Marcy, Nièvre in France. This flight, whose insignia (that of SAL 17) was a leopard rampant with a devil's head (here painted white when normally it was red), was subsequently re-equipped with Potez 63.11s.

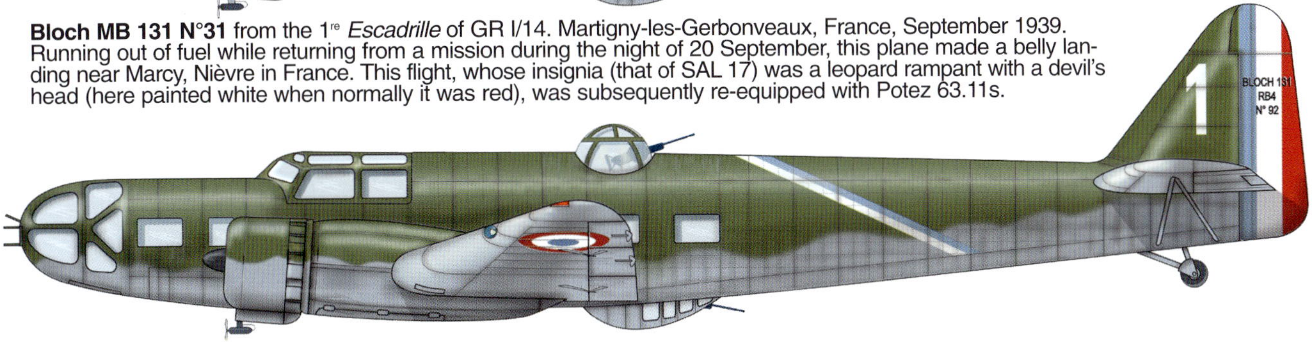

Bloch MB 131 N°65 from the 2e *Escadrille* of GR I/14. Martigny-les-Gerbonveaux, September 1939. This unit received its planes in the spring of 1939 and carried out operational missions only at the beginning of the war, and then at night. The 2nd Flight's insignia in this group was that of the former C 53 and consisted of a "tierced band with oblique white on blue" painted diagonally on the fuselage.

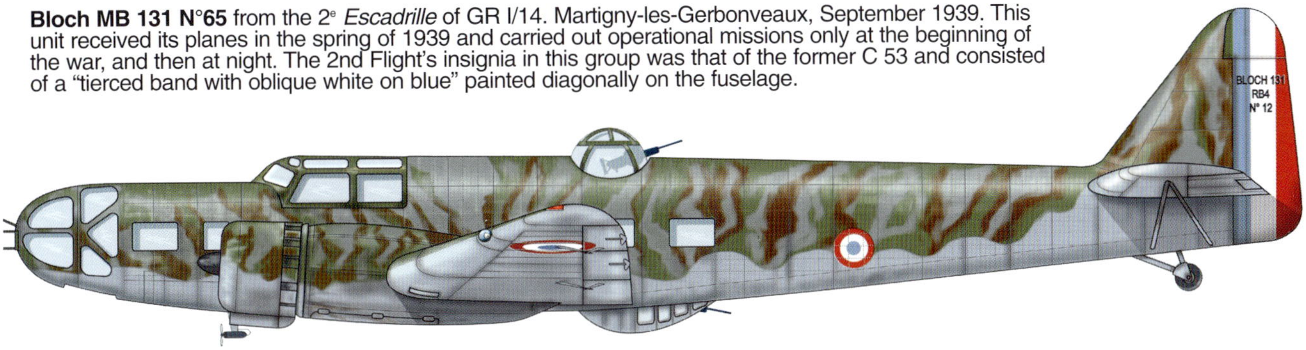

Bloch MB 131 N°12 from the *Centre d'Instruction au Bombardement* (CIB – Bomber training centre) at Toulouse, damaged at Castres on 1 June 1940. This plane received rather original extra camouflage on its upper surfaces which had first been painted khaki with a grey blue base, and brown; the lower surfaces were painted light grey-blue with wavy edges, a feature of the MB 131s. The roundels were smaller, especially on the upper wing surfaces - as can be seen on a very well-known period photo - which were non-regulation for the period.

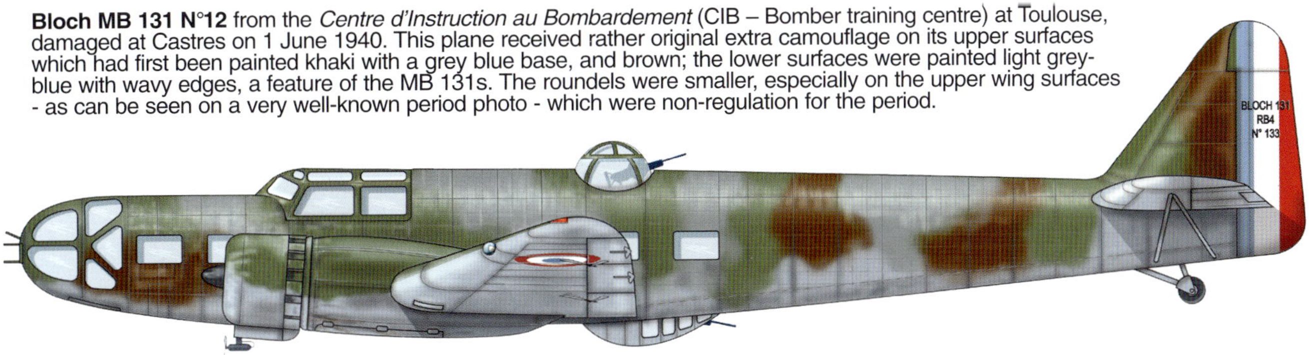

Bloch MB 131 N°133. The MB 131s very quickly confirmed that they had serious failings and were retired from front line service after the first weeks of the war and on 10 May 1940, only one group based in French North Africa was still equipped with them, the other machines having been handed over to training units.

Bloch MB 151 to MB 155

MB 152s from the 3e *Escadrille* of GC II/1. This type of camouflage scheme was typical of planes built at the Marignane plant. *(SHAA)*

The C1 (Single-seat Fighter) Programme submitted to French aircraft manufacturers in 1934 and subsequently modified several times, was intended to replace the machines which were the result of an identical plan launched four years earlier. It required the new fighter to be able, among other things, to reach 250 mph at recovery height. Two types of machines were planned with different engines: either a 800 - 1 000 bhp Hispano-Suiza or Gnôme-Rhône engine, or for the 'light category' called 'C1 Léger' (C1 Light), a 500 bhp Renault, Salmson or Potez engine; the plane could then be built of wood. The altitude it had to be able to reach was 37 950 feet and the armament could consist of either two cannon or four machine guns or even, two machine guns and a canon.

Various projects were submitted among which the Loire 250, the Dewoitine 513, the Nieuport 161, the Morane-Saulnier 405 and the **Bloch MB 150**. The Bloch, which was entered in the first category of the competition, was designed by a team led by the engineer, Mr Roussel. It was made entirely of metal and powered by an air-cooled Gnôme-Rhône 14Kfs radial engine rated at 930 bhp at 14 200 ft. One of its principal characteristics was its very short main undercarriage legs which gave it a very dumpy appearance on the ground. In fact this was not just an impression. When it was decided to go ahead with the first flight, on 17 July 1936, the machine did not even manage to get off the ground!

The project was such a disappointment that it was shelved. Then at the beginning of the following year the Government, having already ordered the MS 405, had the MB 150 project resurrected because it did not want to spread industrial production too much by bringing in yet another manufacturer in view of the difficult political climate at the time. Its wing area was increased and the wing reinforced and the short Bloch undercarriage was replaced by a unit made by the specialist, Messier. A 650 bhp Gnôme-Rhône 14No engine which was a little more powerful was installed. Thus re-equipped, the new Bloch MB 150 N°1 flew for the first time at last on 29 September 1937. Sent to the CEMA for official trials, the plane, although unstable when diving or landing, was easy to handle, but it was clearly underpowered: at the end of the same year, it could only reach 271 mph with great difficulty.

At the beginning of 1938, new modifications were made to the prototype (lengthened wings, larger wingspan, increased tail surface, original wing-mounted radiators replaced by a single unit placed between the two wheel wells) and several different power plants were tried out on the airframe among which a Gnôme-Rhône 14 N-7. At the end of these trials, three prototypes intended to test different types of engines (Gnôme-Rhône and Pratt and Witney) and designated respectively MB 152, MB 153 and MB 154 were ordered in January 1938; in April a second order was placed for 25 pre-production machines with an option for a further 450, to be delivered before the end of the following year. These orders were part of the 'Plan V' which, among other things, provided for the delivery of 950 modern planes in less than a year from the beginning of 938. The MB 150 was now included in these plans to back up the MS 405/406 whose production rate was clearly falling behind the schedule. It very quickly became clear that the MB 150 design was not exactly suited to mass production and that the overall design a general needed reworking... So a new, more suitable machine was work out: modified wing profile, wing area reduced to 159.830 sq ft, armament reduced to four machine guns, oil radiator placed under the port wing, tail skid instead of tail wheel and especially a new GR 14 N-11 engine rated at 920 bhp at 12,000 feet. Designated **MB 151**, this new version took to the air for the first time on 18 August 1938 but very quickly overheating problems in the engine occurred: it was badly cooled because it was enclosed in a particularly close-fitting cowling with a very narrow front opening. Apart from this defect, which was only partly corrected with the installation of a different radiator at the beginning of 1939, the new plane was still unstable and still did not meet the original specifications.

Opposite: **The prototype of the MB 150 after some modifications: the undercarriage is still short and the tail smaller than on the following version.** *(SHAA)*

MB 152 N°12 from the 3e Escadrille of GC II/1. The 'Death the Reaper' insignia of the SPA 94 is stencilled on and still pointing forwards. This group obtained 29 kills during the Battle of France. *(SHAA)*

Its successor, the **MB 152** was therefore planned and studied, indeed even as the MB 151 went into production. On one of the MB 151s, a new engine (Gnôme-Rhône 14 N-21) was installed. Two combinations of armament were envisaged: either four 7.5-mm machine guns installed in the wings, or two of these machine guns with two 20-mm cannon - the combination which was almost invariably chosen. This plane flew for the first time on 15 December 1938. A firm order had been placed a few weeks earlier in October (for 432 machines, numbered from 1 to 432 including 407 production series machines and 25 pre-production machines). The plane was given a new power plant (GR 14 N-25) before going for trials at the CEMA in February 1939. Once again, the cooling problems reappeared and forced the designers to study a variety of solutions (more or less open engine cowlings, different size of propeller bosses, etc). Meanwhile, there was no increase in production and by April 1939 only four MB 151s had been delivered. In order to speed things up, it was decided to include the SNCASO factory at Bordeaux-Mérignac in the production schedule but in order not to increase the delay unreasonably, it was decided to fit a 3 1/3 foot-diameter engine fairing on all the initial production series machines. This was a solution which certainly improved the cooling situation but did nothing for the plane's performances... As for the original Gnôme-Rhône propellers, these were replaced by the Chauvière model to reduce delivery delays.

In conformity with the original order, two airframes were used for different power plant trials. MB 152 N°434 was thus given a Pratt and Witney R-1830 Twin Wasp and a Hamilton propeller which made it the **MB 153**; another machine, the **MB 154**, was to have been fitted with a Wright engine, but this project was stillborn.

In May 1939, 22 MB 151s and 152s came off the production lines and ten had been delivered to the Armée de l'Air; since new defects had appeared, it was urgently decided that the MB 151s would be assigned to training missions. The 144 machines of this type were therefore shared out as follows: 85 to the training units, 30 to the *Aéronavale*, 25 to the Greek Air Force and finally four left at the disposal of the SNCASO for tests. The production of the 488 MB 152s was divided in two principal groups:

MB 151 seen at Toulouse after the Armistice: the machine gun trap doors are open and the propeller boss is missing. *(Archives WM)*

TECHNICAL SPECIFICATIONS (MB 151)

Type
Single seat fighter
Power plant
One 14-cylinder Gnôme-Rhône 14 N-11 or N-35 radial engine rated at 895 bhp at take off (920 bhp at 9 900 feet) and driving a three-blade metal Gnôme-Rhône propeller.
Dimensions
Length: *30 ft.*
Height: *13 ft.*
Wingspan: *34 ft 4 in.*
Wing Area: *186.415 sq ft.*
Unladen Weight: *4,566 lbs*
Max. Weight: *6,167 lb*
Performance
Max. Speed: *293 mph at 15,000 feet*
Ceiling: *33,300 ft*
Max. Range : *397 miles*
Armament
Four 7.5-mm MAC 34 machine guns with 300 rounds each.

Below: **The prototype of the MB 151 in flight. Unarmed, its tail is bigger than that of the MB 150.** *(SHAA)*

A line-up of Blochs from the *3ᵉ Escadrille* of GC II/8 seen at Clermont-Aulnat at the end of July 1941. The '14' further to the rear is one of the rare MB 155s used by this group. *(ECPA)*

- the first two hundred machines (N°9 to 300) with a Gnôme-Rhône 14 N-25 (or 39) engine rated at 920 bhp at 9,900 feet, a 3 ft 4 in engine fairing opening and exhaust manifolds fitted with flame dampers.

- the following 288 machines (N°301 to 431, N° 467 to 500, and N°501 to 696) equipped with a GR 14 N-49 rated at 1,080 bhp on take-off. Just after the war started in September 1939 a so-called 'war order' for a further 500 machines was placed and production rates were speeded up.

All the teething troubles naturally delayed the plane's operational use which anyway was also delayed by the equipment sub-contractors (supplying propellers or armament, etc.) who did not follow the same production schedules as Bloch which itself was on time. It was thus that in September 1939 out of 120 planes delivered 95 did not have propellers…

As for the GC I/1 (the only squadron equipped with the MB 152 at the outbreak of war), even though it had received its new planes at the end of the preceding July, it was eventually mobilised using its old Dewoitine 500s on 27 August 1939 since the new fighters were still not operational… Moreover the pilots were still only luke-warm in their appreciation of the plane. They complained about its delicate handling when diving, even though it turned out to be a very stable gun platform and able to take a good knocking. Nonetheless fighter group conversion continued during the Phoney War and thus GC II/1, III/9, II/10 and III/10 were equipped before the end of 1939. The story goes that nine MB 151s out of 25 ordered were officially supplied to the Royal Greek Air Force at the beginning of the following year.

On 10 May at the start of the German onslaught, GCs I/1, II/1, III/10 (on MB 152) and GC I/10 (on MB 151) were given the defence of the Northern Zone and GCs I/8 and II/8 (MB 152), and GC III/9 (MB 151) the Eastern Zone. GC II/9 was in the process of conversion, and GC II/6 only finished its conversion after the offensive. Moreover, some MB 151s were assigned to the ERCs (regional fighter flights) in order to help their pilots convert to MB 152: ERC 1/561 and 2/561 which became GC II/10 in January 1940; ERC 1/562 - the future GC III/9 -and finally 3/561 and 4/561 – the future GC III/10.

Between the 10 and the 31 May more than a hundred MB 152s were supplied to the Armée de l'Air followed by a further 84 machines in the first six days of June. When new units made up of Polish pilots were created and entrusted with the defence of sensitive points (factories, towns, etc.), the MB 151s came back into active service again. In all up to the end of the campaign, the Armée de l'Air received 632 Bloch fighters: 140 MB 151s, 482 MB 152s, nine MB 155s and one MB 153. At the end of the Battle of France 80 MB 152s had been lost of which eight by accident, as well as four MB 151s (two in combat) for a score which totalled 150 kills with 35 probables. GC I/1 held the unit record (36 kills and four probables) with *Sergent* Teillet and *Capitaine* Coutaud in particular, respectively 7 kills and 1 probable and 6 kills and 2 probables. This was far from being a ridiculous tally especially considering how long it was before the planes were operational. Their lack of range having prevented them from crossing the Mediterranean to reach French North Africa, more than 300 machines (51 MB 151s, 259 MB 152s, nine MB 155s and the MB 153 prototype) were left in the Unoccupied Zone after the June 1940 Armistice.

Three fighter squadrons (GC II/6, II/10 and III/10) were disbanded in July-August 1940 and six others were officially allowed to continue to use the MB 152 with an average of 24 machines per Unit: GC I/1 at Lyon-Bron, II/1 at Le Luc-en-Provence, I/8 at Montpelier-Fréjorgues, II/8 at Marseille-Marignane, II/9 at Clermont-Ferrand-Aulnat and finally III/9 at Salon-de-Provence. As the D.520 was chosen as the 'standard' fighter in 1941, three squadrons (GC I and II/1, III/9) were converted to this type in June 1942.

At the end of November 1942 at the time of the German invasion of the Unoccupied Zone, several dozen machines (170 out of a total of 300 of all variants of which 80 were operational) were seized by the Germans who used them as trainers and gave some of them to Rumania.

TECHNICAL SPECIFICATIONS FOR MB 152 (MB 155)

Type

Single seat fighter

Power plant

One 14-cylinder Gnôme-Rhône 14 N-25/then 14 N-49 (14 N-49) double row radial engine rated at 1 130/1 180 bhp (1100 bhp) at take off and 1 000 bhp/1070 (1000 bhp at 9900 feet) at recovery height, driving a three-blade metal Gnôme-Rhône or Chauvière propeller.

Dimensions

***Length:** 30 ft.*
***Height:** 13 ft.*
***Wingspan:** 34 ft 4 in.*
***Wing Area:** 186.415 sq ft.*
***Unladen Weight:** 4,620 lb (4,708 lb).*
***Max. Weight:** 6,160 lb (6,380 lb).*

Performance

***Max. Speed:** 301 mph/318 mph at 16 500 feet (325 mph).*
***Ceiling:** 33,990 ft/36,465 ft (38,742 ft)*
***Max. Range at 18,150 feet:** 362 miles/337 miles (656 miles).*

Armament

Two 7.5-mm MAC 34 machine guns and two 20-mm Hispano-Suiza HS 404 cannon with 60 rounds each.

Opposite: **MB 151 N°37 from GC III/10 in flight. The plane does not bear any flight insignia or fuselage roundel. The shape of the air intake under the cowling and the absence of wing-mounted cannon were typical of this version.** *(SHAA)*

While manufacturing was still in progress – it stopped at the time of the Armistice with N°699 – an improved version, the **MB 155** was started by the SNCASO. This was nothing more than a touched up MB 152 – the definitive version, some have said... - whose central and front fuselage structure had been modified (wider engine cowling) with a newer, larger fuel tank, which had forced the designers to move the cockpit further back in order to keep the same centre of gravity. The Gnôme-Rhône 14 N-49, used for the last batches of the MB 152, was kept and the horizontal tail surfaces bracing struts were removed. For the first time on a French machine, an armoured windshield and belt-fed (instead of drums) cannon were fitted.

The first production series MB 155 made its first flight on 3 April 1940 but only ten machines were finished by the time of the Armistice (N° 701 to 710, the last two being destroyed on the ground) although the authorities had ordered 400 machines. Production of the MB 155 also ceased with the Armistice but 19 airframes in the process of being assembled (N°711 to 729) were nevertheless finished, all the machines serving alongside the MB 152s and eventually being assigned to GC I/8 except for N° 708 which became GC II/8's commanding officer's plane.

The Bloch fighter line started with the MB 150 and finished with the MB 157 prototype which carried out a few trials in 1942 at the request of the Germans. Its design went back to 1939 when the Gnôme-Rhône 14 R 'Météore' engine came out and which the SNCASO had intended to fit into an MB 152 air frame, calling it the **MB 156**. This installation could not be carried out without greatly modifying the machine, especially because of the weight of the power plant. So it was decided to design a new plane (a more ovoid fuselage, longer undercarriage legs with a wider track, etc.) under the leadership of Lucien Servanty in order to get the best out of the intended engine and obtain its 1 700 bhp; this was the **MB 157**, armed with two cannon and four machine guns. The arrival of the Germans in Paris prevented the prototype from being assembled and it was loaded onto a trailer and shipped to Poitiers. This load was intercepted on route and stocked in the SNCASO factory at Mérignac which was in the German-controlled part of the country. When assembly was completed, the plane finally took off in March 1942 and carried out a whole series of tests at the beginning of 1943 during which it was decided to ferry the plane to Orly where its engine was dismantled in order to be tested in a wind tunnel. The story of this promising fighter, which some have called the 'French Thunderbolt' and whose performances were very close to those that other piston-engined fighters reached but only in the last stages of the war, ceased abruptly when the airframe which had been stored in an airship hangar at Orly was irretrievably damaged in an air raid.

Above: **The MB 152 was the first fighter of this type to be received by GC I/8 in November 1939. The camouflage scheme is quite characteristic of the plane and can be seen clearly.** *(SHAA)*

Below: **MB 151 N° 108 from GC III/10 at the beginning of 1940. The plane does not bear any flight insignia, whereas the serial number has been painted on the fuselage, behind the roundel.** *(SHAA)*

Bloch MB 151 & 152

Bloch 151 N°58 (Ser. N°Y-545) from the 3e *Escadrille* of GC II/10. Rouen-Boos, France, November 1939. GARC 561 was previously equipped with Dewoitine D.501s and became GC II/10 on 11 January 1940, entrusted with the air cover of the Lower Seine region; it started its war operations the following day. The insignia of this plane which was damaged on 11 April 1940 is that of the '*Cercle de Chasse de Paris*' – the Paris Fighting Circle.

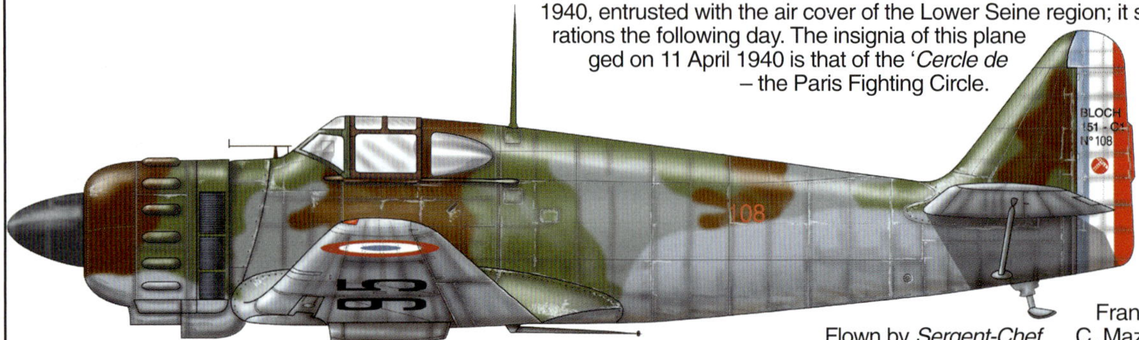

Bloch 151 N°108 (Ser. N°Y-595) from the 5e *Escadrille* of GC III/10. Le Havre-Octeville, France, January 1940. Flown by *Sergent-Chef* C. Mazo. N°108 was one of the first MB 151 delivered to this unit in December 1939 and it replaced the ancient NiD 622 biplanes and Blériot-SPAD 510s… It was destroyed in a belly-landing on the following 14 May.

Bloch 151 N°364 (Ser. N°Y-851) from the CIC (Fighter Instruction Centre) at Chartres, France, March 1940. This plane was flown by *Caporal-Chef* Karel Posta, a Czech pilot in the Armée de l'Air who joined up after the invasion of his country by the Germans. The Donald Duck armed with a club was the insignia of one of the flights of CIC N°6 and can be found on three other planes. In May 1940 a defence patrol was created at Chartres with Czech pilots trained there.

Bloch 152 N°111 (Ser. N°Y-598) from the 1re *Escadrille* of GC I/1. Chantilly, France, 10 May 1940. This was Captain Couteaud's personal aircraft; he was the flight commander, one of the three greatest French aces on MB 152 during the Battle of France with six kills and two probables to his credit.

NB: In order to make the page lay-out easier, the ventral antenna has been shown folded up on these aircraft where it was naturally down in flight.

Bloch MB 152

Bloch 152 N°134 (Ser. N°Y-621) from the *2e Escadrille* of GC I/1. Chantilly, France, Spring 1940. Like this plane, all the MB 152s with a GR 14 N-25 engine and a 3 ft 4 in-diameter engine cowling still in service were handed over to other groups at the end of April 1940 (mainly GC II/10) and replaced by machines with a 14 N-49 engine and a 2 ft 10 in cowl.

Bloch 152 N°175 (Ser. N°Y-662) from the *2e Escadrille* of GC I/1. Chantilly-les-Aigles, France, May 1940. This plane, a 'former' GC I/8 plane, was considered lost after its pilot, *Lieutenant* Schmidt, belly landed it at Berneuil-sur-Aisne on 16 May 1940.

Bloch 152 N°649 from the *3e Escadrille* of GC II/1. Buc, France, May 1940. The *1re Escadre de Chasse* (GC I/1 and II/1) was one of the first wings to receive the Bloch fighters and was entrusted with defending the northern zone on 10 May 1940.

Bloch 152 N°539 from the *3e Escadrille* of GC II/1, Brétigny-sur-Orge, France, June 1940. This plane was abandoned at Buc on 2 June 1940.

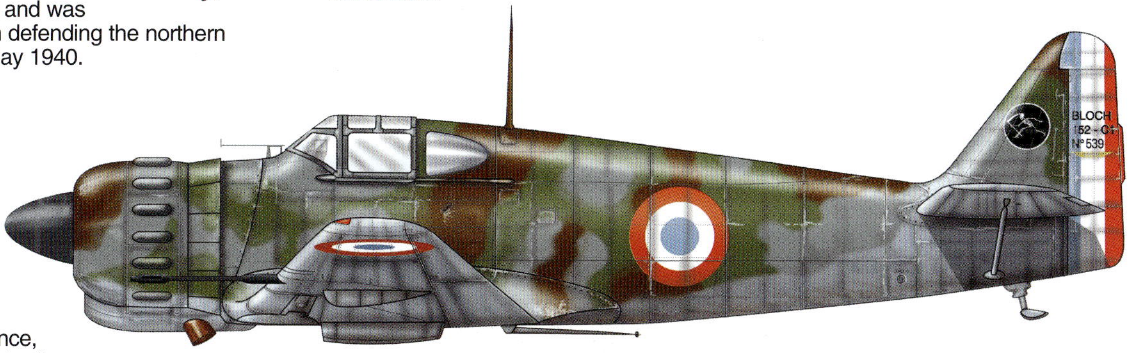

Bloch MB 152

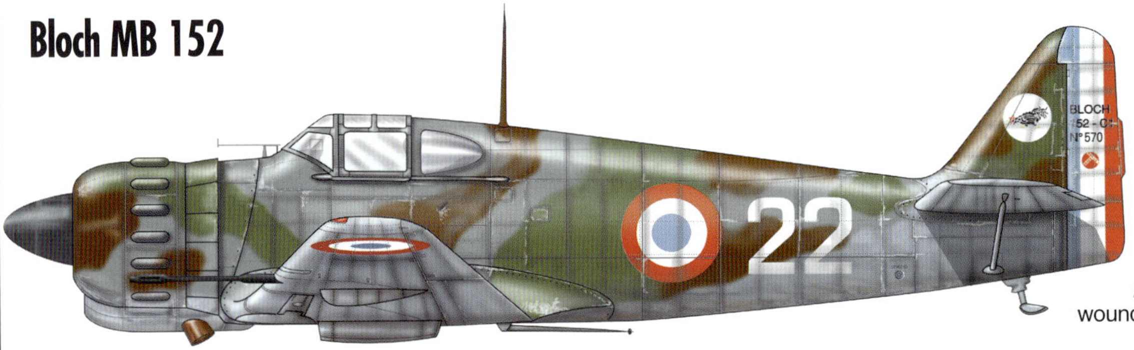

Bloch 152 N°570 from the *4e Escadrille* of GC II/1. This fighter was lost in aerial combat on 14 May and its pilot, *Sous-Lieutenant* Maurin, wounded in the engagement.

Bloch 152 N°136 (Ser. N°Y-623) from the *4e Escadrille* of GC II/1. Couvron, France, May 1940. *Sergent-Chef* Roquerbe returned to his airfield with his plane so badly shot up that it was in eventually abandoned.

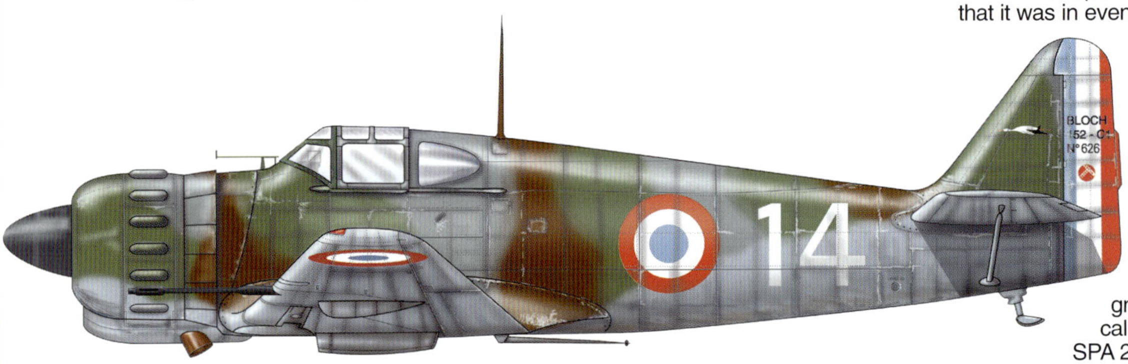

Bloch 152 N°626 from the *3e Escadrille* of GC II/6. Toulouse, France, June 1940. The flight's small insignia (the flying stork called 'St. Galmier' of SPA 26) was painted on the tail according to the regulations.

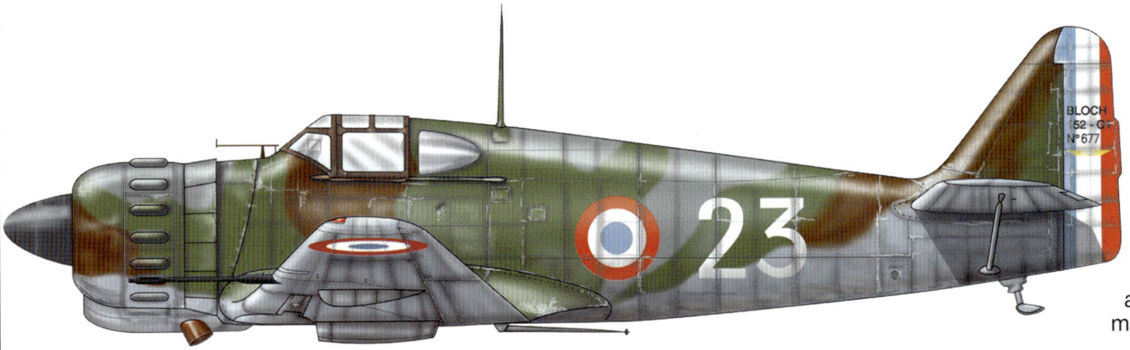

Bloch 152 N°677 from the *4e Escadrille* of GC II/6. Anglures-Vouarce, France, June 1940. This plane was shot down during a dogfight on 6 June; its pilot, *Sergent* Geillon, although wounded, managed to bail out.

Bloch MB 152

Bloch 152 N°634 from the *4ᵉ Escadrille* of GC II/6. Toul, France, 24 June 1940. This plane bore the nickname 'Tyts' on the right-hand side, given to the pilot, *Sergent* Philippe d'Elbée, by his wife.

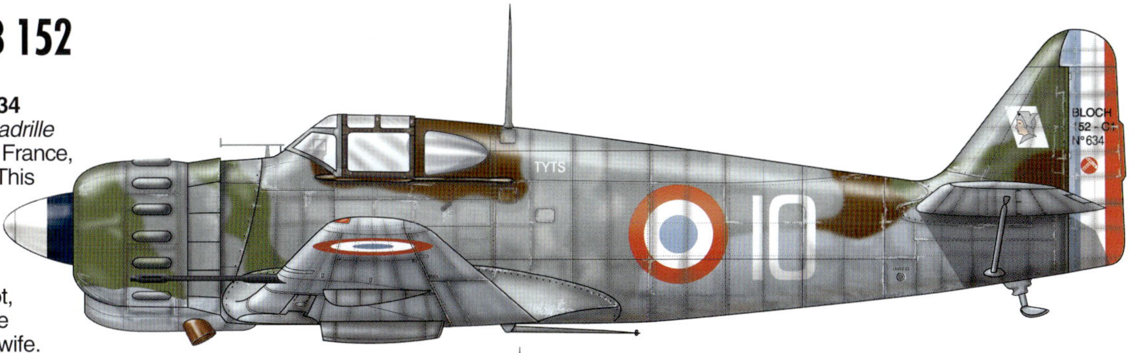

Bloch 152 N° 231 (Ser. N°Y-718) from the Staff of GC I/8. Hyères-les-Palmiers, France. Apart from a fuselage roundel which was of an unusual size, this plane has the Ace's tri-colour stripe round the fuselage its pilot, *Commandant* Marc Ambrogi, being a WWI ace with 14 kills. The personal insignia on the tail of this plane, one of the first three delivered to this group on 20 November 1939, shows 'Dopey' the dwarf from the cartoon 'Snow White' which was particularly popular in France at the time; he is playing the flute, the pilot's favourite instrument! As one can see, the Staff planes had no individual number, in theory at least.

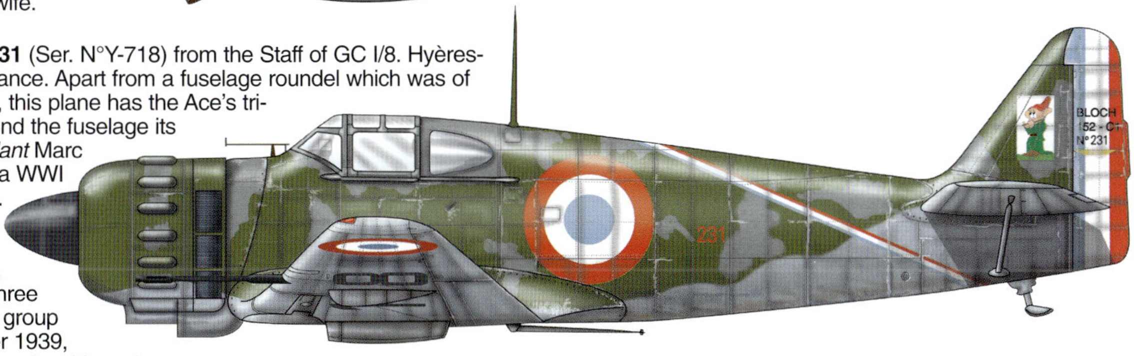

Bloch 152 N°641 from the *1ʳᵉ Escadrille* of GC I/8. Brétigny-sur-Orge, France, June 1940. This group was created from the Navy *Flottille de Chasse* 3C2 transferred to the Armée de l'Air in January 1936 and has an insignia which recalls its origins: a winged trident ending with a curve and a sailor's knot.

Bloch 152 N°329 (Ser. N°Y-805) from the *3ᵉ Escadrille* of GC II/8. Marseilles, France, December 1940. During the Battle of France, this plane bore the individual number '6'. The insignia showing an 'attacking shark' is due to the fact that this flight, formerly the French Navy '*Flottille de Chasse*' 3C1, was transferred to the Armée de l'Air in January 1936.

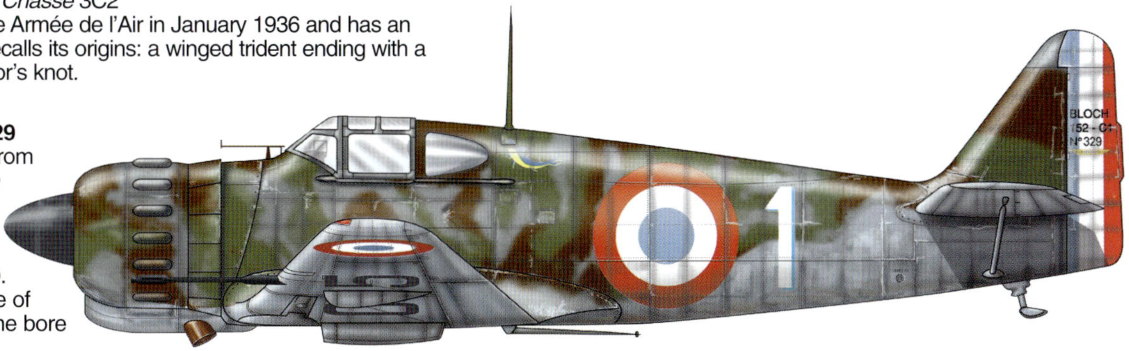

Bloch MB 152

Bloch 152 N°562 from the *3e Escadrille* of GC II/8. Aix-les-Milles, France, June 1940. This fighter squadron operated briefly from Lympne in England on 30 May during the encirclement of allied troops in the Dunkirk pocket.

Bloch 152 (N°unknown) from the *4e Escadrille* of GC II/8, Marseille-Marignane, France, 1940. Note the amazing diversity that existed in the individual numbers on MB 152s. On the planes in this unit, the number was first painted like here, on a white disk then after October 1940, in large white figures behind the fuselage roundel.

Bloch 152 N°639 from the *4e Escadrille* of GC II/8. Marseille-Marignane, France, 1942. This plane had a particularly long life since it ended its career in 1947! In this flight, the planes were numbered from 15 to 26 from October 1940.

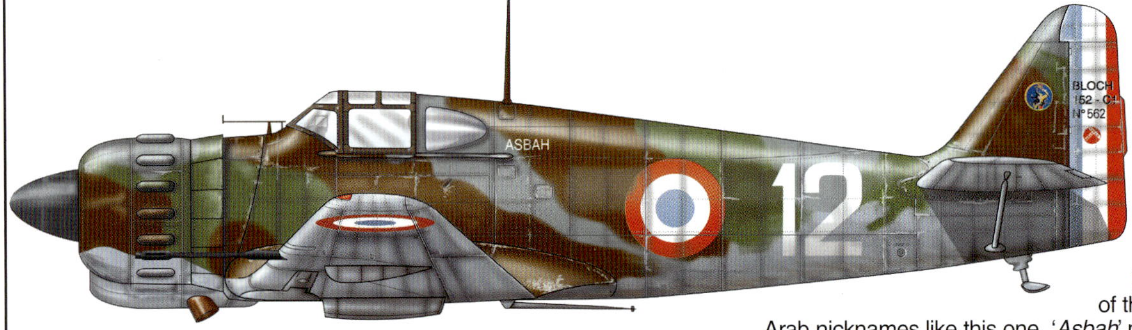

Bloch 152 N°562 from the *3e Escadrille* of GC II/9, Clermont-Aulnat, France, August 1940. This group being originally set up in French North Africa, some of the planes received Arab nicknames like this one, '*Asbah*' meaning 'morning'.

Bloch MB 152

Bloch 152 N°499 from the *3e Escadrille* of GC II/9. Connantre, France, May 1940. Numbering in this flight (N° 40 to 5-) was changed from 1 January 1941, the planes having an individual number from 1 to 12.

Bloch 152 N°617 from the *3e Escadrille* of GC II/9. Clermont-Aulnat, France, end of 1940. The nickname '*Cave Caudam*' ('beware of the tail' in Latin) worn on both sides was only added after this plane was transferred; it previously was in GC III/10.

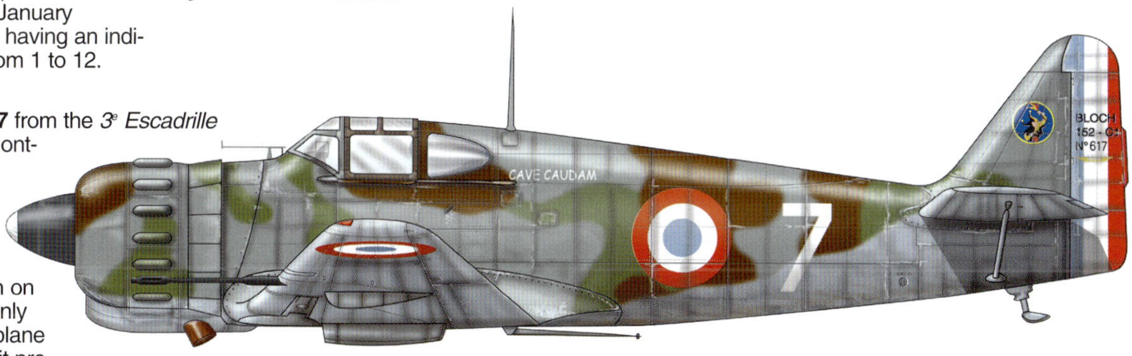

Bloch 152 N°251 from the *3e Escadrille* of GC II/9. Clermont-Aulnat, France, June 1942. Note the peculiar, mainly yellow logo, a feature of the planes built in the Bordeaux factory and which – in theory – were given the uneven numbers. Although this plane, and the following one, were among the MB 151/152s which were given their underside serial number (up to N° 432), we have not shown this as it only appeared later.

Bloch 152 N°166 from the *3e Escadrille* of GC II/9, Clermont-Aulnat, France, end of 1942. The markings on this plane were the last worn by the Vichy Air Force: fuselage roundels removed and replaced by a white 'scarf', and tri-colour stripes painted diagonally on the wings. The white tip of the propeller boss is one of the features of the 3rd Flight of this squadron.

Bloch MB 152

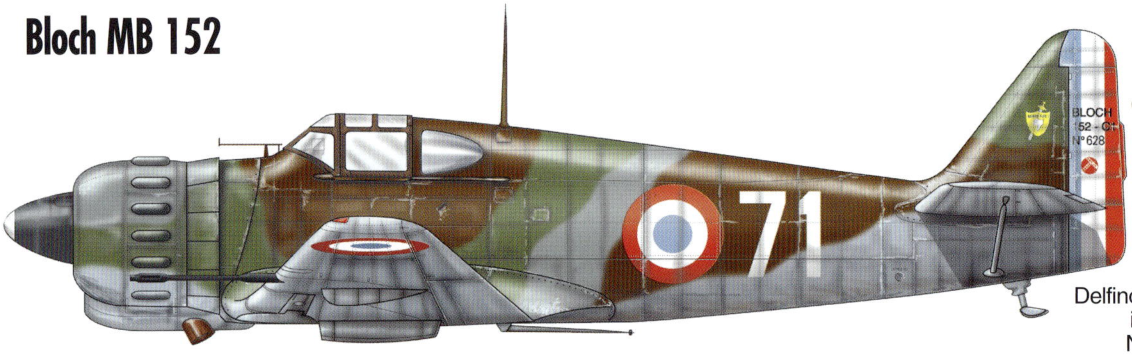

Bloch 152 N°629 from the *4e Escadrille* of GC II/9. Clermont-Aulnat, France, June 1940. This 'White 71' is without doubt the flight commander's plane; *Capitaine* Louis Delfino was a future ace in the 'Normandie-Niémen' squadron.

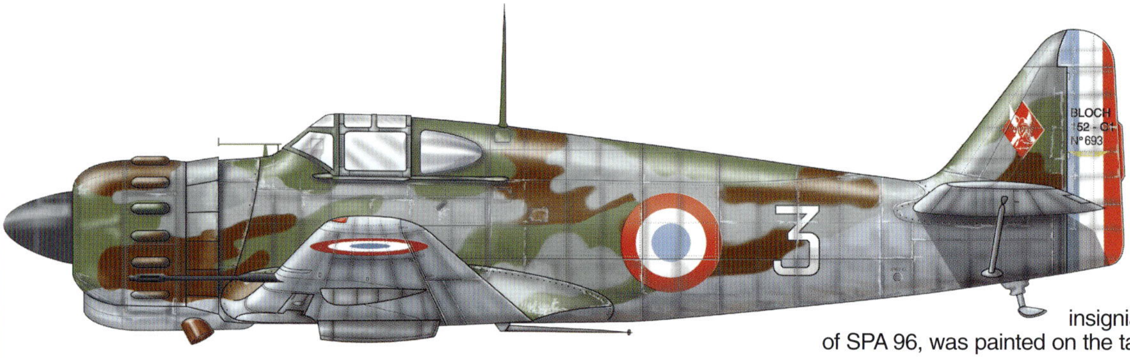

Bloch 152 N°693 from the *6e Escadrille* of GC III/9. Le Luc-en-Provence, France, July 1940. Some of the pilots making up this unit came from the *1re Escadrille* of GC I/6, whose insignia, the Gaul's head of SPA 96, was painted on the tail of the MB 152s.

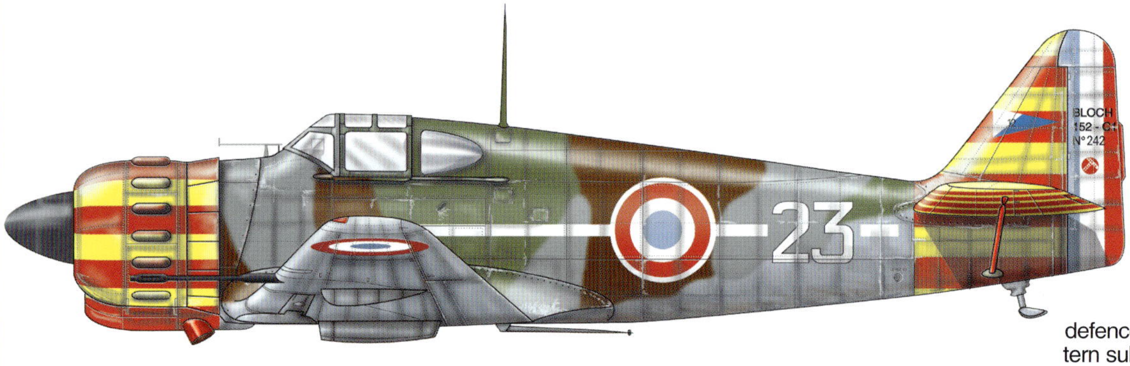

Bloch 152 N°242 from the *6^{e} Escadrille* of GC III/9. Le Luc-en-Provence, France, 1942. Flown by S/Lt Martin. After the Armistice, GCs I/1, II/8 and III/9 made up the *Groupement 22* entrusted with the defence of the south-eastern sub-sector of France.

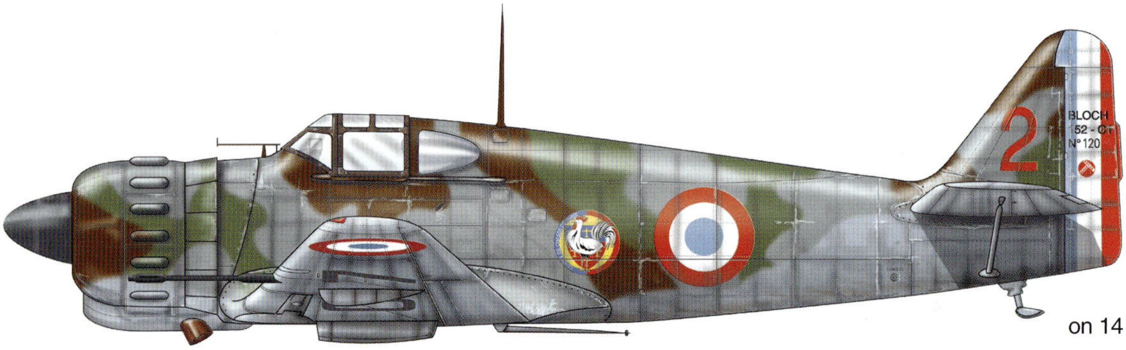

Bloch 152 N°120 (Ser. N°Y-607) from the *4^{e} Escadrille* of GC II/10. Soissons, France, May 1940. It was flown by *Adjudant* Berger when it was shot down by Me 109s on 14 May. The pilot got out unscathed.

Bloch MB 155

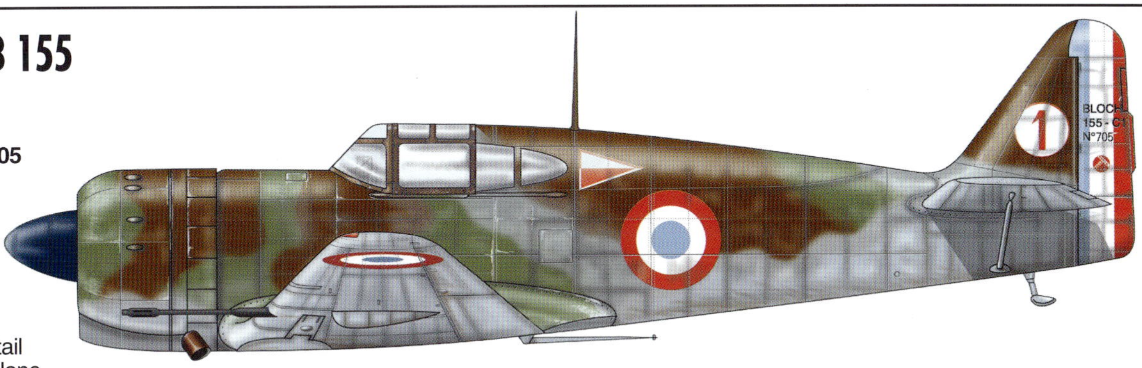

Bloch 155 N°705 from the *4ᵉ Escadrille* of GC II/8. Aix-les-Milles, France, June 1940. As the number '1' painted on the tail indicates, this plane belonged to the commanding officer of the 4th Flight, *Capitaine* Vaublanc.

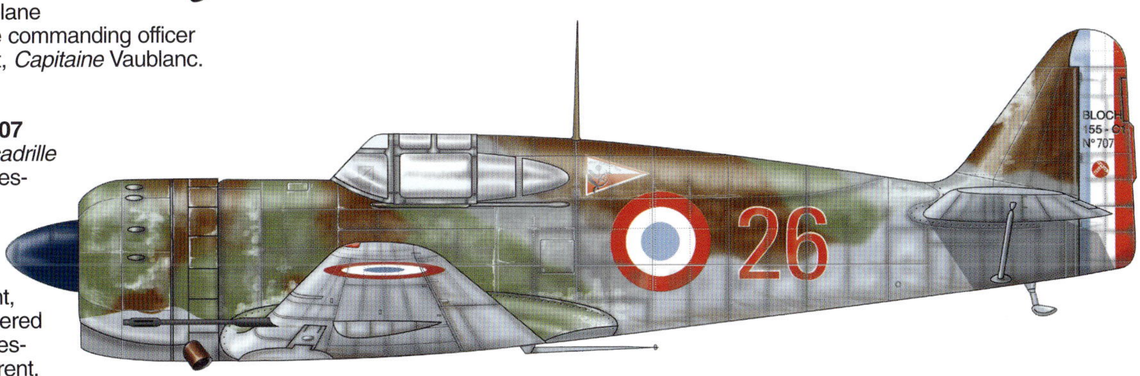

Bloch 155 N°707 from the *4ᵉ Escadrille* of GC II/8. Aix-les-Milles, France, June 1940. Apart from its redesigned front, the MB 155 differed from its predecessors by its different, repositioned cockpit.

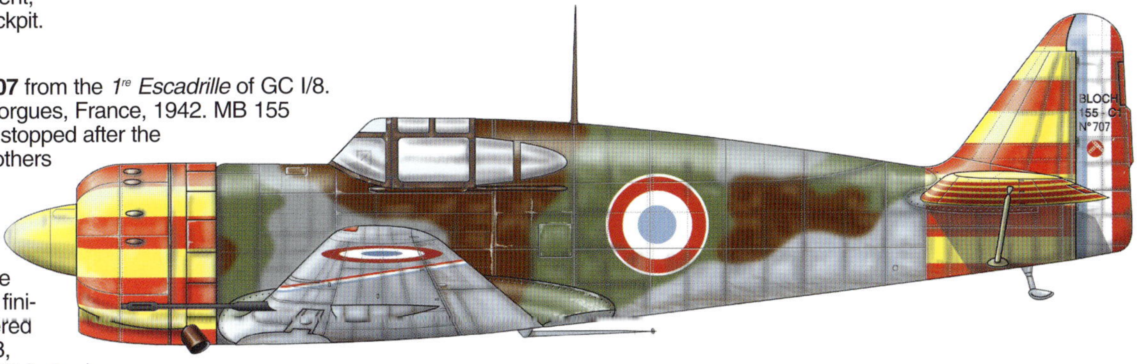

Bloch 155 N°707 from the *1ʳᵉ Escadrille* of GC I/8. Montpellier-Fréjorgues, France, 1942. MB 155 production was stopped after the 8th aircraft, 19 others N° 711-729) in the process of being assembled at the time of the Armistice being finished and delivered mainly to GC I/8, except for N° 708 (below) which became the personal plane of GC II/8's commanding officer.

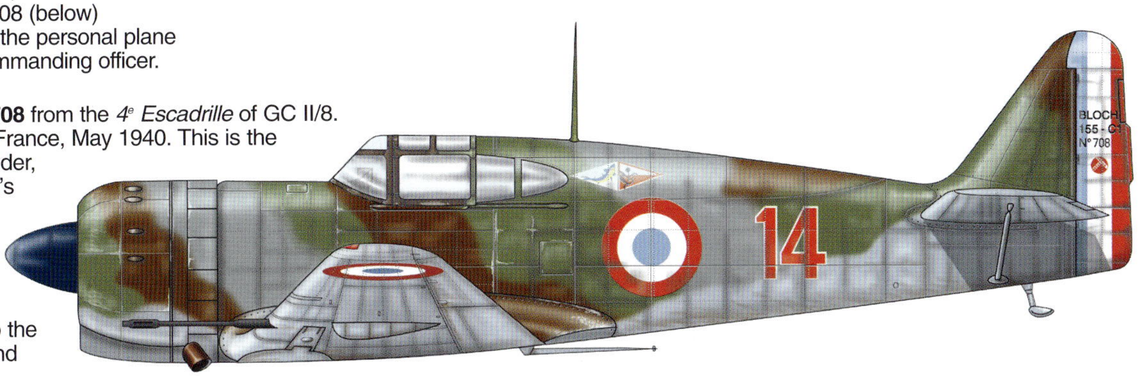

Bloch 155 N°708 from the *4ᵉ Escadrille* of GC II/8. Calais-Marck, France, May 1940. This is the group commander, *Colonel* Robert's plane; that is why it bears the pennants of the two flights which make up the squadron behind the canopy.

Bloch MB 174 & 175

Above: **MB 174 N° 53 from GR II/33 seen here in July 1940 (the insignia on the tail is masked) was used by Antoine de St-Exupéry.** *(SHAA)*

The design of the MB 174, perhaps France's most successful and effective plane during the Battle of France, dated back to the end of 1936. A team from the SNCASO which had just taken over the firm 'Avions Marcel Bloch' after the armament industry's nationalisation programme, started to study the concept of a twin-engined two- or three- seat aircraft for different roles (bombing, reconnaissance, etc.) intended to fill the gap between planes of the B4 category (four-seat bombers), the C3 category (three-seat light twin engined fighters) and the AB2 category (attack and bombing two-seaters) like the Potez 63 or the Breguet 691.

A team headed by Henri Deplante designed the **MB 170** N°01 which flew for the first time on 15 February 1938. This twin-engined aircraft with cantilever wings had a two- or three-man crew housed in a large glazed cockpit in the very front of an ovoid cross-section fuselage entirely made of metal. The wings were typical of the manufacturer with two spars and a small central part which was an integral part of the fuselage and which held the fuel tanks. In spite of the plane's obvious purpose, the bomb bay was relatively small and armament consisted of a 30-mm canon installed in the front left-hand side of the fuselage, two wing-mounted machine guns and two others covering the rear, the one protecting the lower sector being installed in a ventral cupola. This prototype was powered by two Gnôme-Rhône 14 N-6/7 engines and suffered an accident on 17 March 1938, scarcely a month after its first flight; trials resumed with the second prototype, the MB 170B3 N° 02. Designed originally as a fast bomber, this particular aircraft had been extensively modified compared with its predecessor: the ventral cupola used to carry photographic equipment was now useless and was suppressed; the cockpit canopy was enlarged and the portion below the nose was now glazed; the fins were enlarged.

While this N° 02 started its trials, official needs changed and the MB 171, 172 and 173 which were being studied, never got beyond the drawing board. On the other hand priority was given to the strategic reconnaissance version, the MB 174 and the prototype (N°01) flew for the first time on 5 January 1939. Overall, this machine was identical to its predecessors (wings, undercarriage and tail), but the rear canopy was moved further back and the nose was completely glazed in. It was powered by two GR 14 N-20/21 engines. The trials immediately proved to be very promising with the **MB 174** flying 62 mph faster than the Potez 63.11 and 637 from the outset; a contract was signed with the SNCASO on the following 1 February for six pre-series machines and a production series of fifty aircraft. Construction was spread out among the company's factories (wings at Nantes-Bougenais, fuselage and central wing section at Bordeaux-Bègles, etc.) but the final assembly was done at Bordeaux-Mérignac. During new tests the six pre-series machines were given Gnôme-Rhône 14 N-48/49 engines fitted with Bronzavia thrust augmentation exhaust stacks giving an extra 12 mph. The propeller bosses were smaller to improve cooling. The first production series machine (N°7) flew for the first time on 5 November 1939 and deliveries to the Armée de l'Air carried on till the following May. The machines had been put into service during the preceding spring after some modifications carried out on the first examples (machine guns firing rearwards through the lower part of the fuselage, additional armour and twin upper machine guns instead of only one). Contrary to the rather optimistic estimates, getting the MB 174 operational was delayed so much that at the beginning of May 1940, only 52 machines had been delivered out of the total order for 271 aircraft. GR II/33 had the privilege of being the first user of the machine, three machines reaching the unit on 19 March 1940; they were very quickly thrown into the fray since their first mission was on the 29th of the same month, led by the famous *Capitaine* Antoine de Saint-Exupéry. The other groups gradually received their MB 174s, respectively GR II/36 and I/35.

Although there were not very many of them (less than fifty), these planes nevertheless played an important role, carrying out important strategic reconnaissance missions by getting away from enemy aircraft by flying fast and high up. At the time of the Armistice, in June 1940, 25 machines had survived and were all regrouped in GR II/33 based at Tunis-El-Aouina, the only group allowed to carry on using this type; a small number of machines were captured by the Germans and served briefly as trainers in the Luftwaffe. These twin-engined aircraft came back into service briefly after when they went over to the Allies during the Tunis Campaign; in 1942 a pylon was fitted enabling a 550- or 1100-lb bomb to be carried.

With the MB 174 being a success right from the first tests, it was decided to stop production of this model after the fiftieth

machine and to put everything into a bomber version, the **MB 175**. For the plane to correspond to its new role, the bomb bay had to be enlarged. This was a delicate operation because of the wing spars which were integral with the fuselage.

This was entirely redesigned and the spars moved so that the internal volume of the bomb bay could be increased by 15%, which lengthened the aircraft by 6-inch. The rest of the machine on the other hand remained unchanged. Although the prototype had not yet made its maiden flight, an official order for 814 MB 175s and 323 **MB 176**s, identical to the 175 but powered by Pratt and Witney Twin Wasps (a way of saving on Gnôme-Rhône 14 N engines which at the time were in great demand for French fighters), was placed in September 1939. This programme was reviewed in February 1940. 660 MB 175 were supposed to come off the production lines, along with 1 550 MB 176s, between April 1940 and July 1941. The MB 175 N°01, the prototype, flew for the first time in December 1939 and the first production series machine (MB 175B N°01) the following April, before being delivered a month later to GR II/52 which was a... reconnaissance unit! In all, this unit received twelve machines of this type before the 19 June 1940. Apart from these planes, out of the twenty MB 175s built before the Armistice, two were given to GAO 510 (another reconnaissance unit) and the remainder were left in the depots. GR II/52 went over to North Africa and was the only group authorised to continue flying on MB 175 after making up its strength by taking machines which were waiting ready at Bordeaux (including some MB 176s) and flying them across the Mediterranean individually. These machines ended their careers on the base at Oran, November 1942 in the fighting during Operation 'Torch'.

Above, left: **A camouflage scheme with parallel stripes was painted onto several MB 174s as seen here on N°30, during trials at the beginning of 1940.** *(SHAA)*

Above: **From the outside, the MB 175 was very much like the Bloch 174 although the longer bomb bay had lengthened the fuselage by six inches or so.** *(DR)*

As for the production of the MB 176, it was finally especially limited because of the difficulty in getting hold of American engines. This variation (the first production series machine N°201 came out in May 1940) performed slightly better than its counterpart. Five machines were built before production ceased because of the Armistice; there were about 200 airframes at different stages of completion.

Production of the MB 175 was taken up by the Germans in 1940-1941 and the planes sent to Germany where they were mainly used to train Luftwaffe pilots. During this period, an **MB 177** had been envisaged. It was a similar plane but powered by Hispano-Suiza 12 Y31s whose installation necessitated extensive modifications to the engine frames; the engine was a disappointment as it was underpowered. Among the variants envisaged, it is worth mentioning the **MB 175A** which could carry two 1100 lb bombs or a torpedo slung under the belly, but only a wooden model was made of this aircraft; the **MB 175B**, a two-seat heavy fighter intended to replace the Potez 631, with more powerful Hispano-Suiza supercharged engines and armed with two 20-mm cannon and four machine guns in the nose; and finally the high-altitude bomber, the MB 178 which was being built at Courbevoie when the factory was overrun in June 1640.

TECHNICAL SPECIFICATIONS

Type
Twin-engined three-seat reconnaissance bomber
Power Plant
Two 14-cylinder Gnôme-Rhône 14 N-48 (left)/ 49 (right) air-cooled radial engines rated at 1140 bhp at take-off.
Dimension
Length: *40 ft.*
Height: *11 ft 6 in.*
Wingspan: *58 ft 9 in.*
Wing Area: *405.011 sq ft.*
Unladen Weight: *12,320 lb.*
Max. Weight: *15,730 lb.*
Performance
Max. Speed: *331 mph*
Range: *1125 miles*
Ceiling: *36,300 ft.*
Armament
Two 7.5-mm MAC machine guns in the wings with 1000 rounds each. Twin MAC machine guns for rear defence; one then three MAC 34s for the rear lower defence sector; 880 lb of bombs carried internally (MB 175 = 1320 lb.).

MB 174 N° 53 from GR II/23 in flight above North Africa. The plane bears Vichy markings on the engines and the tail as well as the name 'Joane' under the windshield, hidden here by the reflection. *(SHAA)*

Bloch MB 174

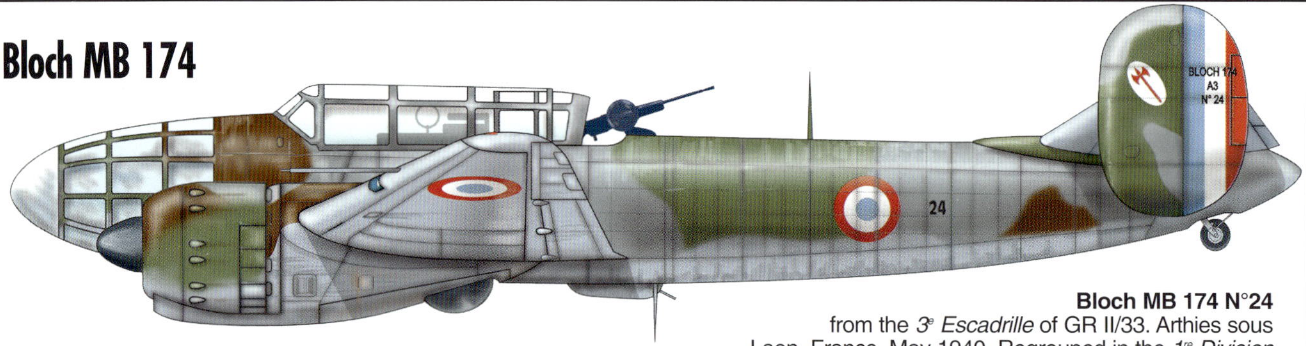

Bloch MB 174 N°24 from the *3ᵉ Escadrille* of GR II/33. Arthies sous Laon, France, May 1940. Regrouped in the *1ʳᵉ Division Aérienne* with the *Groupes de Bombardement* of the ZOAN, this unit only had two of these modern twin-engined planes on 10 May 1940, serving alongside the Potez 637 or 63.11. It was in these ranks and on this type of plane that Antoine de St-Exupéry served, telling his story in the book '*Mission to Arras*'.

Bloch MB 174 N°25 from the *2ᵉ Escadrille* of GR II/33. Tunis-el-Aouina, Tunisia, summer of 1940. After GR II/33 was disbanded in the summer of 1940, the 3rd and 4th Flights of GR II/33 became respectively the 1st and 2nd.

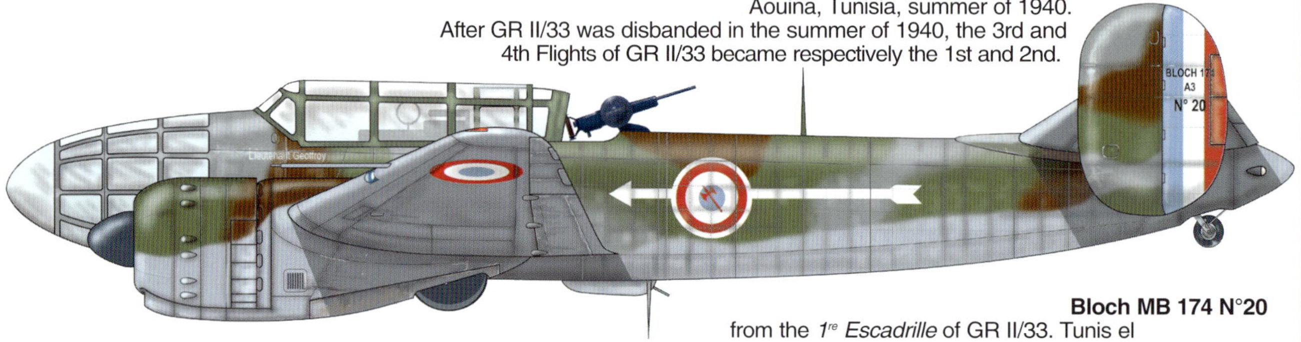

Bloch MB 174 N°20 from the *1ʳᵉ Escadrille* of GR II/33. Tunis el Aouina, Tunisia, 1941. Christened 'Lt Geoffroy' after the observer of a Potez 637 shot down on 5 November 1939, this plane bears the unit insignia (a 'boarding axe' of SAL 33 after a pun based on the name of one of its commanding officer's name, *Capitaine* A. Bordage) painted in a not very regulation way directly onto the fuselage roundel.

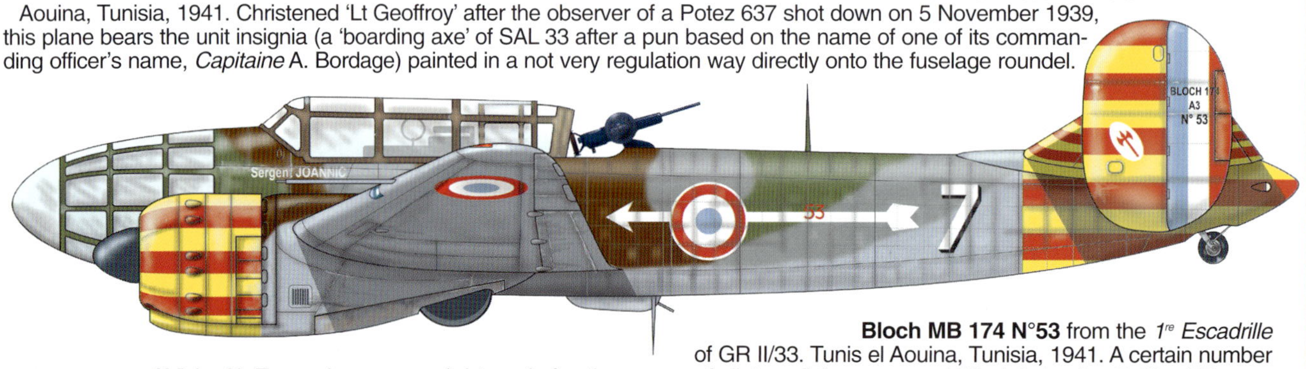

Bloch MB 174 N°53 from the *1ʳᵉ Escadrille* of GR II/33. Tunis el Aouina, Tunisia, 1941. A certain number of Vichy Air Force planes were christened after the names of pilots or flying personnel killed during the Battle of France. Thus, this MB 174 was named after 'Sgt Joannic', a machine gunner killed on 12 May 1940.

Bloch MB 174 & 175

Bloch MB 174 N°30 from the 3ᵉ *Escadrille* of GR I/52. St-Dizier, France, May 1940. The squadrons equipped (only partly) with MB 174s during the Battle of France were very few in number but they carried out strategic reconnaissance missions of undoubted value. As can be imagined, the planes were rarely given an insignia let alone an individual number.

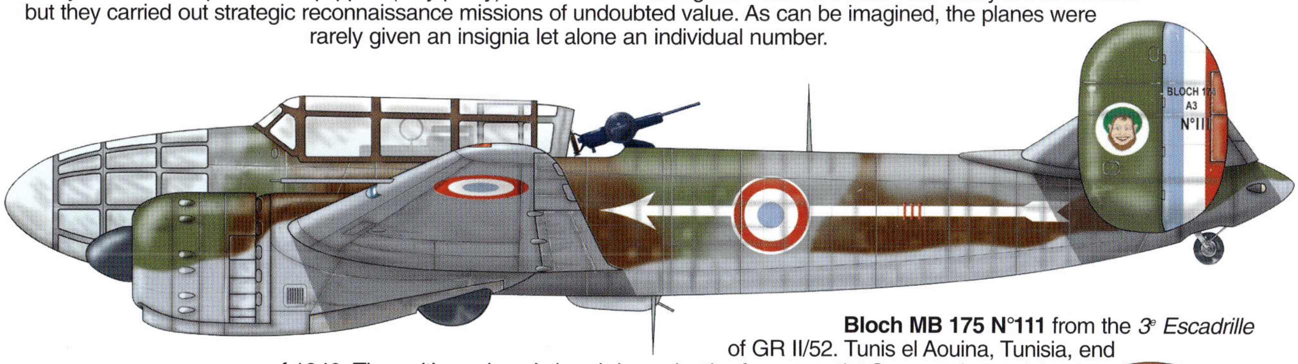

Bloch MB 175 N°111 from the 3ᵉ *Escadrille* of GR II/52. Tunis el Aouina, Tunisia, end of 1940. The unit's coalman's head drawn by the famous artist Sem can be explained by the fact that it came from and was based at Clermont-Ferrand.

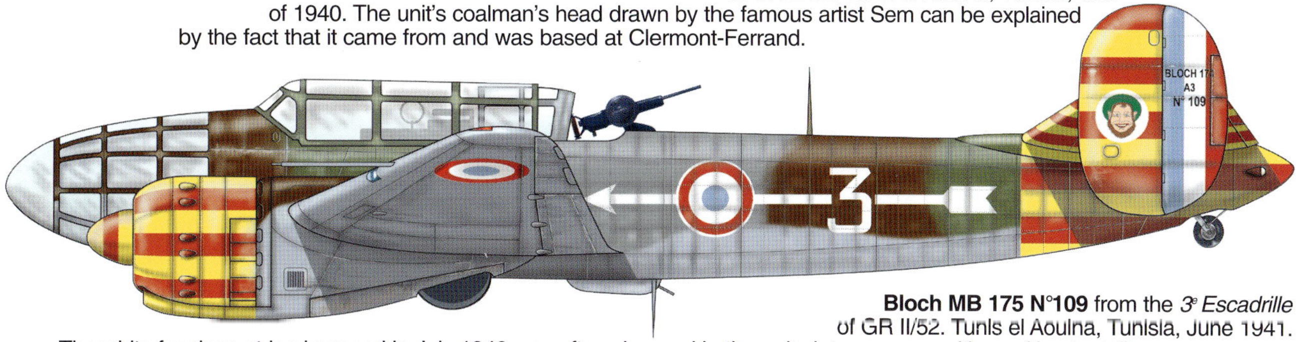

Bloch MB 175 N°109 from the 3ᵉ *Escadrille* of GR II/52. Tunis el Aouina, Tunisia, June 1941. The white fuselage stripe imposed in July 1940 was often changed in the units into an arrow with or without a tail, as here. As for the instructions concerning the Vichy stripes dated 24 June 1941, they were also interpreted in different ways. In theory the propeller boss was supposed to be red.

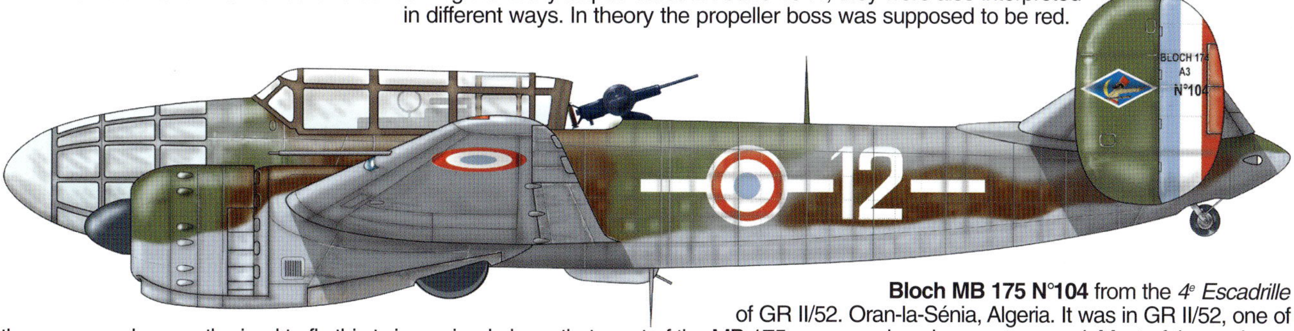

Bloch MB 175 N°104 from the 4ᵉ *Escadrille* of GR II/52. Oran-la-Sénia, Algeria. It was in GR II/52, one of the rare squadrons authorised to fly this twin-engined plane, that most of the MB 175s ever produced were regrouped. Most of these planes were destroyed on the ground during allied raids during Operation Torch, the Allied landings in French North Africa, on 8 November 1942.

Bloch MB 200

Above:
A group of Bloch MB 200s from the 2e Escadrille of GB I/39 in flight. The insignia painted according to the regulations on the fuselage can be seen quite clearly. The three planes have been entirely painted dark green (called 'tableau' green, and often by mistake 'émaillite' (bright)green.) except for the engine cowlings which have been left bare metal colour. The armament of the aircraft in the foreground (N°88 has not been installed, but the bomb-launcher pylons can be seen under the fuselage, as can the Pitot tube in the form of a trident under the front and the strange trim tab sticking out from on the rudder.
(Coll J. Delmas)

When the war started in September 1939, the MB 200 was the oldest French bomber in service, its design going back to 1928. It was the result of a programme intended, among other things, to replace the LeO 20 biplanes; it was later modified in 1930 and 1932, the prototype of the multi-seat day and night bomber making its maiden flight in June 1933 powered by two Gnôme-Rhône 14 Krds engines. It was sent for tests to the CEMA the following September where it was modified (various reinforcements). This four-seat high-wing monoplane built entirely of metal and possessing a fixed undercarriage could carry 2 640 lb of bombs over 625 miles and reach 175 mph with a full load.

A first official order was placed in December 1933 for 30 machines of which 26 were built by Potez, whose factories were better tooled than those of 'Avions Marcel Bloch'. The first production series MB 200 which was fitted with 870 bhp Gnôme-Rhône GR 14 Kirs engines, flew in September 1934, twenty of these planes being accepted by the Armée de l'Air at the end of the year. Until the middle of June 1935, several extra contracts were signed bringing the total number to a little more than two hundred aircraft, made by a number of manufacturers (Hanriot, Loire, Breguet and Potez) whereas licence-built machines in Czechoslovakia were made by Aero and Avia.

In May 1935, the first 38 MB 200s delivered went to equip GB I/12 and II/12 based at Rheims as well as GC II/22 at Chartres. At the end of the following year, 179 of the 197 planes built were in service of which 120 in the *1er Corps Aérien Lourd* (First Heavy Air Corps) and 24 in the eight fighter groups as 'fighter command machines'. In fact using them like this, a sort of FAC or AWACS before their time was eventually abandoned as it obliged the MB 200s to direct the fighters in full view of the enemy, a situation which made them particularly vulnerable...

In September 1939, although their replacement had often been intended and even provided for, 92 MB 200s out of a total of 169 were still in the line in the seven bomber groups, of which four were in Metropolitan France (GB I/31 and II/31, and I/32 and II/32). The losses suffered by the 31e and 32e *Escadres* in the first weeks of the conflict sped up the ancient twin-engined aircraft's retirement from front line service, the units still equipped with them falling back to Lézignan and Orange, in the south, a long way from the fighting, where they could be converted to more modern aircraft (e.g. LeO 451 and DB-7). From then on, the MB 200 was reserved for training units, except for the Syrian Campaign (May-July 1941) when a flight from the Levant (EAB – *Escadrille Autonome de Bombardement 3/39*) created on 1 September at Aleppo with the planes from GB III/39, took part in the fighting in June 1941.

Unlike some of its contemporaries, the MB 200 only gave rise to two variants, both made privately by Bloch:

- the MB 201 of which two were built was similar to the production series MB 200 and fitted with 690 bhp Hispano 12 Ybrs water-cooled engines.
- the MB 202 was a four-engined version (powered by four GR 7Kdrs 350 bhp engines which flew in 1934 but which was finally retired three years later.

TECHNICAL SPECIFICATIONS

Type
Four-seat bomber

Power plant
Two 14-cylinder air-cooled Gnôme-Rhône 14 Kirs radials developing 870 bhp.

Dimensions
Length: *52 ft 10 in.*
Height: *12 ft 10 in.*
Wingspan: *74 ft 1 in.*
Wing Area: *721.121 sq ft.*
Unladen Weight: *9843 lb.*
Max. Weight: *16,016 lb.*

Performance
Max. Speed: *178 mph at 14,190 feet.*
Max. Range: *625 miles.*
Practical Ceiling: *23,100 feet*

Armament
Three 7.5-mm MAC 1934 machine guns (one in the front and dorsal turrets and one flexible mounted in the ventral position), 1980 to 2640 lb of bombs.

Bloch MB 200

Bloch MB 200 N°82 (Ser. N°E-117) from the *1re Escadrille* of GB I/32, Dijon-Longvic, France, September 1939. This squadron carried out a number of combat missions (armed reconnaissance) at the beginning of the war with this type of machine before being sent to the rear to be converted onto Douglas DB-7s.

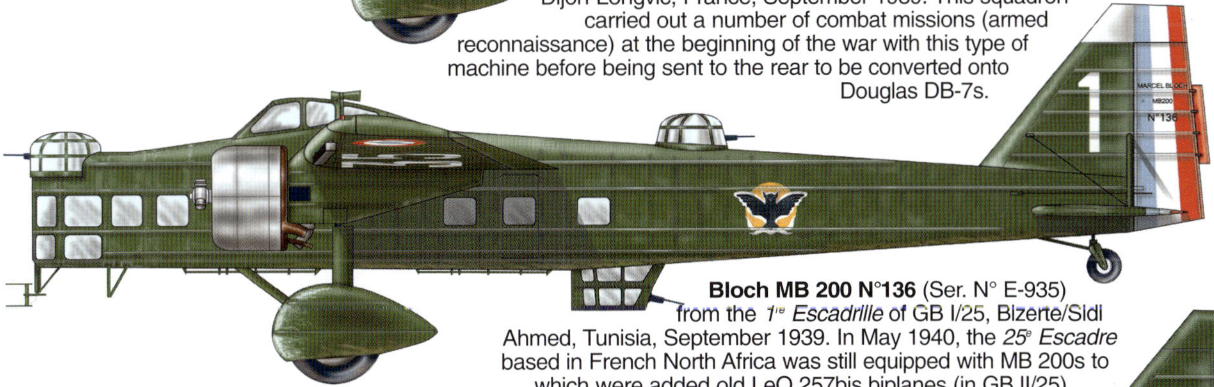

Bloch MB 200 N°136 (Ser. N° E-935) from the *1re Escadrille* of GB I/25, Bizerte/Sidi Ahmed, Tunisia, September 1939. In May 1940, the *25e Escadre* based in French North Africa was still equipped with MB 200s to which were added old LeO 257bis biplanes (in GB II/25)…

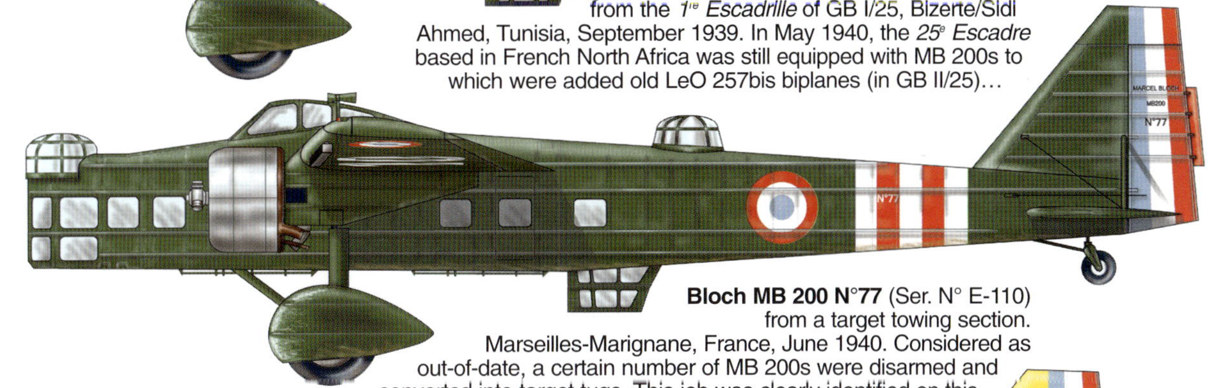

Bloch MB 200 N°77 (Ser. N° E-110) from a target towing section. Marseilles-Marignane, France, June 1940. Considered as out-of-date, a certain number of MB 200s were disarmed and converted into target tugs. This job was clearly identified on this machine by the red and white stripes round the fuselage; otherwise it was painted the '*tableau*' green, the usual colour for French pre-war bombers.

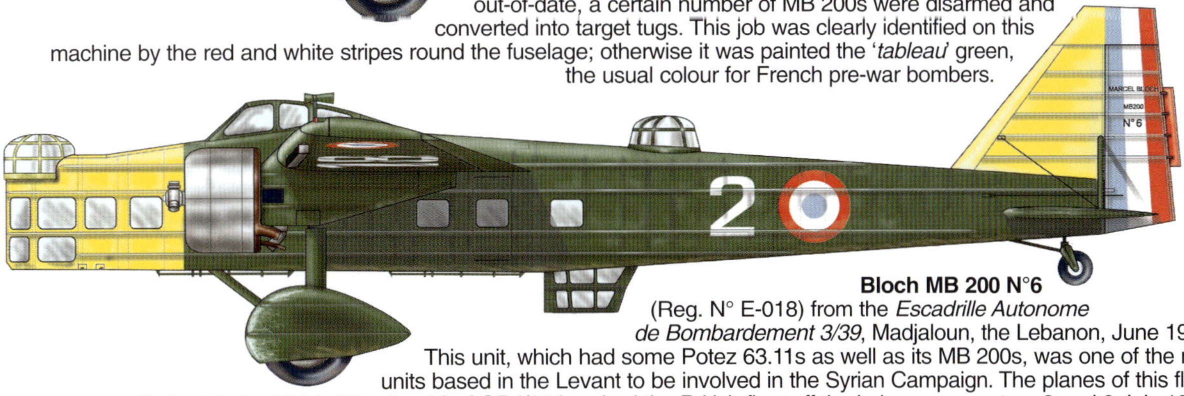

Bloch MB 200 N°6 (Reg. N° E-018) from the *Escadrille Autonome de Bombardement 3/39*, Madjaloun, the Lebanon, June 1941. This unit, which had some Potez 63.11s as well as its MB 200s, was one of the rare units based in the Levant to be involved in the Syrian Campaign. The planes of this flight together with the Martin 167Fs (Marylands) of GB I/39 bombed the British fleet off the Lebanese coast on 8 and 9 July 1941; the surviving Blochs and the Potez 25 TOEs coming from the reconnaissance flights made up a night bomber group but this did not last long.

Bloch MB 210

Above: **Bloch MB 210 N°22 (Ser. N° E-364) of the 2^e^ *Escadrille* of GB I/19. In August 1939, this squadron found itself in Algeria where it was converted to DB-7 the following year.** *(SHAA)*

The MB 210 was a direct descendant of the MB 200 from which it borrowed its entirely metal construction and angular, extensively glazed fuselage; in a way it represented the transition stage between the older braced high-wing bombers with fixed undercarriage – like the Amiot 143 – and modern machines with cantilever wings and retractable undercarriage (LeO 451, Amiot 351, etc.). Built on the personal initiative of Marcel Bloch in answer to an official request for a night bomber which could eventually double as a torpedo bomber and replace the LeO 20 series, a first prototype, the MB 210 N°1 flew for the first time on 23 November 1934 equipped with Gnôme-Rhône 14 Kdrs/grs Mistral Majors developing 800 bhp each. At the same time a second prototype was built, called the MB 211 and equipped with two 860 bhp Hispano-Suiza water-cooled engines; it was shown at the *Salon de l'Aéronautique* in 1934 before flying for the first time on 29 August 1935. It had been modified like the first prototype at the end of the preliminary trials: tail plane changed, the dorsal turret repositioned.

A first official contract for 80 MB 210s to be made by Bloch, Potez and Hanriot was signed the same year, the first of the production series machines flying on 12 December 1935. Although it was fixed on the prototype, the landing gear on the production series machines was retractable; the power plant had been improved (GR 14 Kirs/jrs installed in more faired nacelles) and defensive armament now consisted of three turrets equipped with 7.5 MAC machine guns. A walkway arranged in the centre of the bomb bay separated it in two. A modification was made after the second series machine giving a larger positive dihedral angle to the part of the wing situated outboard of the engine nacelle. At the end of 1936, 181 extra machines were ordered and this time, other builders (Renault, ANF-Les Mureaux and Breguet) were co-opted into the construction of the aircraft. Thanks to new contracts awarded in 1937 to the SNCAO, SNCASO and SNCAC which had just been created by the nationalisation of the armaments industry the previous year, the total of MB 210 to be built rose to 257 machines (253 for the Armée de l'Air and 54 for Rumania) which were delivered until the month of August 1938.

GB II/21 was the first squadron to receive the new bomber in November 1936 but its beginnings turned out to be rather disappointing. Indeed the planes were under-powered and there were several accidents due to engine overheating and seizure, which caused the MB 210 to be called the 'Flying Coffin' by its crews... The planes were grounded and only took to the air after being fit- ...ith new engines (GR 14 N-10/11), better cooled and slightly more powerful (650 bhp). These engines had already been tried out in the summer of 1937.

When the war started, 238 MB 210s were still in service in Metropolitan France in the 11e, 12e, 19e, 21e, 23e and 51e *Escadres de Bombardement* which each regrouped two squadrons of between 13 and 16 machines. The *19e Escadre* - GB I/19 and II/19 - which was initially based at Bordeaux-Mérignac, was transferred to North Africa (Morocco then Algeria) in May 1939 and only returned to the mainland after converting to the DB-7 in April 1940.

With the Amiot 143, this twin-engined bomber was the mainstay of the French bomber force but like its companion it was very quickly out-of-date. After having carried out reconnaissance missions and a few night sorties, as a precaution it was decided to remove it from the front line units and use it for crew conversion whilst waiting for more modern types.

This conversion was not in fact always completed given the delays in delivering the new planes and that is why several units – like those equipped with the Amiot 143 – were obliged to launch 'mixed' groups into battle consisting of modern bombers and MB 210s, or even only MB 210s, often the only bomber available...

TECHNICAL SPECIFICATIONS

Type
Twin-engined five-seat bomber

Power plants
Two Gnôme Rhône 14 N-10/11 air-cooled radial engines developing 910 bhp at take-off and 950 bhp at 12,000 ft

Dimensions
***Length:** 62 ft 1 in.*
***Height:** 22 ft 2 in.*
***Wingspan:** 75 ft 3 in.*
***Wing Area:** 774.936 sq ft.*
***Unladen Weight:** 14,080 lb.*
***Take-Off Weight:** 21,318 lb.*
***Max. Weight:** 22,440 lb.*

Performance
***Max. Speed:** 201 mph at 11,550 ft.*
***Cruising Speed:** 172 mph at 13,035 ft*
***Max. Range:** 812 miles with 3300 lb of bombs.*
***Max. Ceiling:** 32,670 ft.*

Armament
Three 7.5-mm MAC 1934 machine guns (one in the turret in the nose, one in the retractable dorsal turret and one in the turret under the belly) and 3 520 kg of bombs

Above: **Bloch MB 210 N°102 ? (Ser. N° E-449 ?) seen at Istres after the Armistice. Note the indispensable long access ladder for the front position.** *(Coll. Vincent Gréciet)*

The *11e Escadre* was an excellent example of this situation: although GB I/11 was equipped with LeO 451s on 10 May 1940, GB II/11 was mobilised in September 1939 at Istres in order to counter an possible attack by Italy (which in the end remained neutral) and started to receive its new bombers in the following December. But the conversion was not finished by June 1940 when Italy entered the war and the raids carried out, notably against the FIAT factories in Turin, consisted of mixed groups, made up of LeOs and MB 210s. Finally from 18 June onwards all the machines which were still available fell back across the Mediterranean.

The *12e Escadre* on the other hand was far better equipped since its two squadrons, GB I/12 and II/12, after being quickly transferred from Eastern France to Caen in Normandy were re-equipped with LeO 451s at the end of October and the end of 1939 respectively.

The *21e Escadre* was to have been equipped with the new Amiot 351/354s. For this, its two squadrons (GB I/21 and II/21) were sent south to Avignon, the first becoming the experimental unit for the new bomber. But the conversion had not quite been completed when the Germans attacked on 10 May 1940; GB I/21 only had six Amiots which were put into operation alongside its six old Blochs.

It received reinforcements during the following weeks but these consisted of rather worn out MB 210s with which a good number of missions were nonetheless carried out (harassing motorised columns, dropping equipment and supplies to the encircled troops in the Dunkirk pocket on 30 May) before the surviving machines fell back to North Africa after 19 June.

23e Escadre was a particular case as, although its first squadron (GB I/23) did actually receive the intended Leo 451s in February 1940, it had to pass them on to other units and as a result found itself with only two of these planes on the following 15 May! Its main force consisted of some MB 210s which were supposed to have been used for training and to which were joined by further machines of the same type. The age of the planes however caused the number of accidents to increase so the squadron did not carry out any more combat missions and waited for the supposed LeO 451 replacements. GB II/23 was luckier since after being sent to the south of France to get used to the new planes, it flew LeO 451s only when sent back to the Paris region (Etampes) on 2 June 1940.

Finally the fate of the *51e Escadre* was totally different as its two squadrons (GB I/51 and II/51) which had received their MB 210s in 1938 carried out night missions (armed reconnaissance, dropping leaflets, etc.) at the beginning of the Phoney War and were then sent to the base at Luc-en-Provence in December 1939 where they converted to Breguet 691/395 *(cf. p. 58 foll.)* after a training course on Potez 633 from January 1940 onwards.

Once the Armistice was signed, all the surviving machines (120 aircraft) were mothballed and some even scrapped. GBs I/21 and II/21 were disbanded during the summer of 1940. The MB 210 was no longer considered as a bomber and went on to be a target tug, six machines being used by the *Ecole de l'Air* at Salon-de-Provence. When the Unoccupied Zone was finally invaded in November 1942, the Germans seized the 37 surviving examples of this twin-engined plane…

Bloch MB 210 N°1 (Ser. N° E-341) during trials. The plane, nicknamed 'Verdun' was equipped with an asymmetrical probe and its propellers have bosses. *(Coll. Vincent Gréciet)*

Bloch MB 210

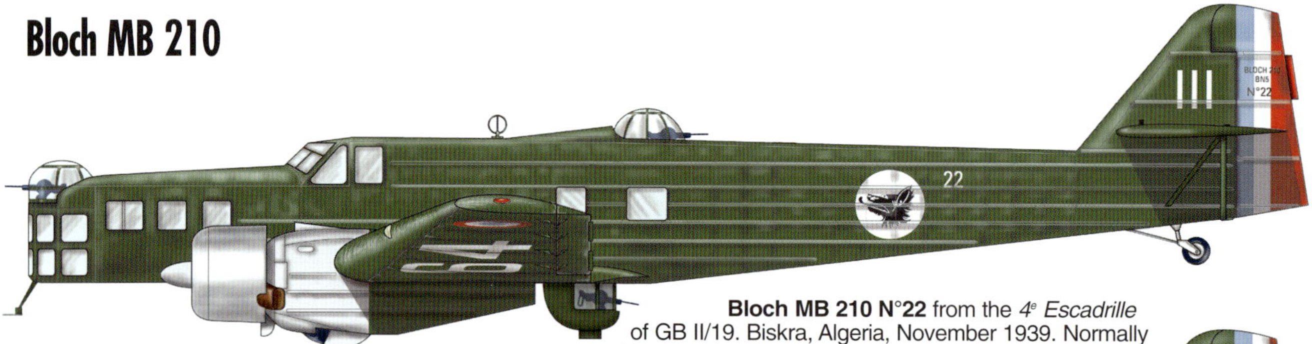

Bloch MB 210 N°22 from the *4e Escadrille* of GB II/19. Biskra, Algeria, November 1939. Normally based at Bordeaux-Mérignac, the two squadrons of the *19e Escadre de Bombardement* were sent to French North Africa in May 1939 and only came back to France at the end of the following May, after having converted to Douglas DB-7.

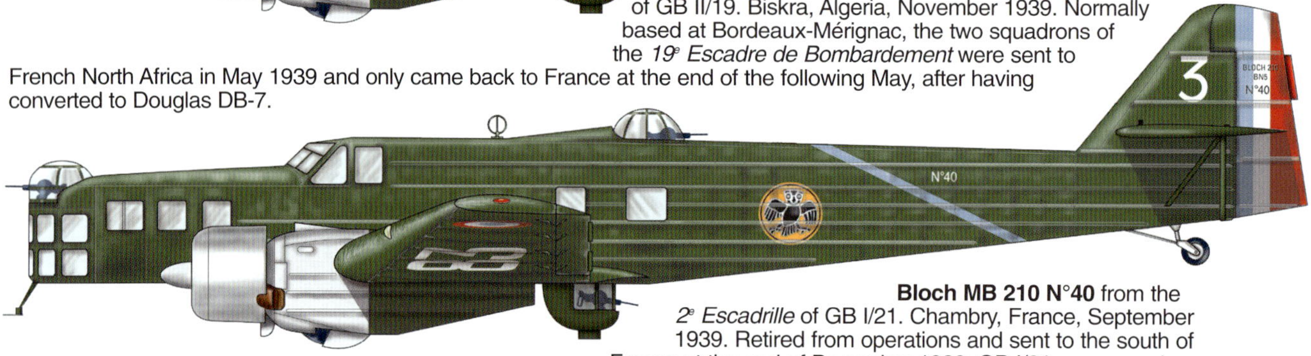

Bloch MB 210 N°40 from the *2^e Escadrille* of GB I/21. Chambry, France, September 1939. Retired from operations and sent to the south of France at the end of December 1939, GB I/21 never received its whole batch of Amiot 351/354s and had to carry out its operational missions aboard its MB 210s and whose number had to be made up in May 1940 with machines from other units and quite clearly already quite 'worn out'…

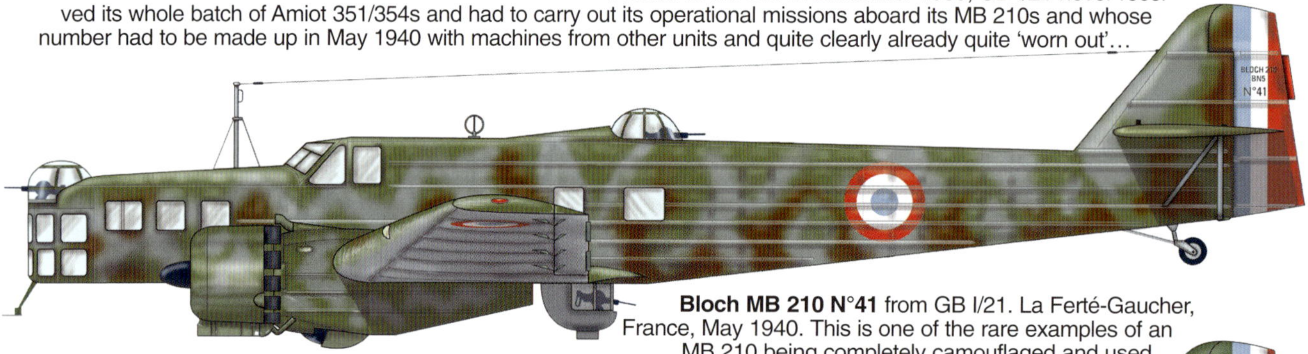

Bloch MB 210 N°41 from GB I/21. La Ferté-Gaucher, France, May 1940. This is one of the rare examples of an MB 210 being completely camouflaged and used operationally during the Battle of France. From 4 to 10 June, GB I/21 carried out bombing missions against the German motorised columns on these out-of-date, and often out-of-breath too, machines before falling back to French North Africa from 19 June onwards.

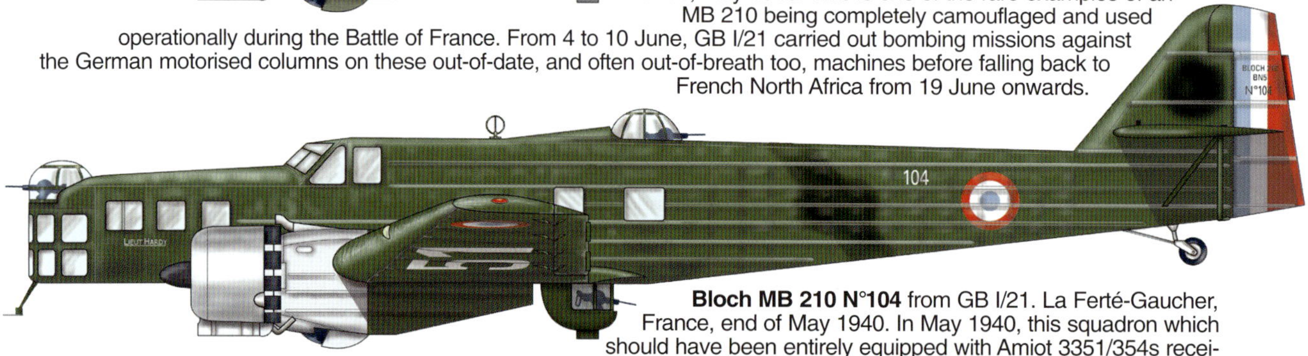

Bloch MB 210 N°104 from GB I/21. La Ferté-Gaucher, France, end of May 1940. In May 1940, this squadron which should have been entirely equipped with Amiot 3351/354s received a certain number of MB 210s to complement the ones it already had originally; they were handed over by units which no longer had any use for them. This is the case of this plane, a former GB I/51 machine as shown by the insignia and the hastily covered fuselage stripe; it was called '*Lieutenant Hardy*' and was destroyed during an air raid on its air field on 24 May 1940.

Bloch MB 210

Bloch MB 210 N°14 from the *4e Escadrille* of GB II/21. Laon-Nangis, France, September 1939. This plane was hit by flak on 25 May in the Soissons region as it was on its way back from a night bombing mission. All the crew perished in the crash that followed.

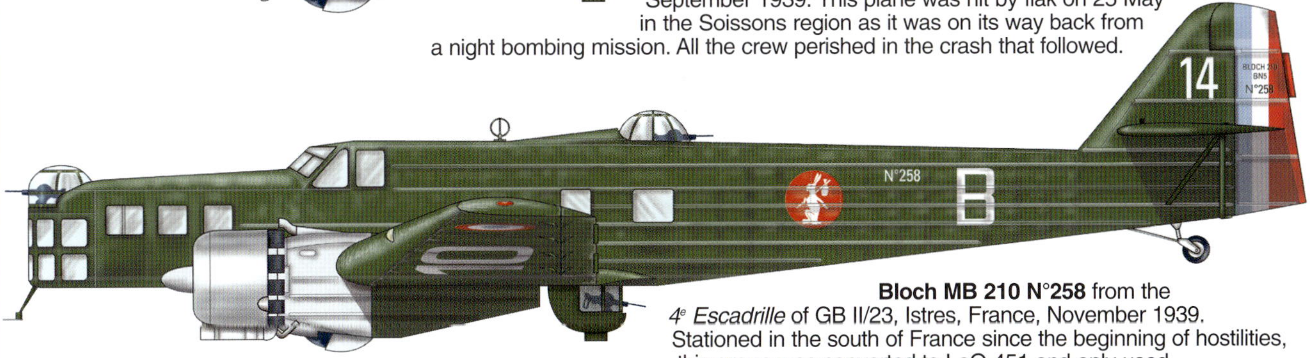

Bloch MB 210 N°258 from the *4e Escadrille* of GB II/23, Istres, France, November 1939. Stationed in the south of France since the beginning of hostilities, this group was converted to LeO 451 and only used the new bombers went it moved north to join the combat zones at the beginning of June 1940.

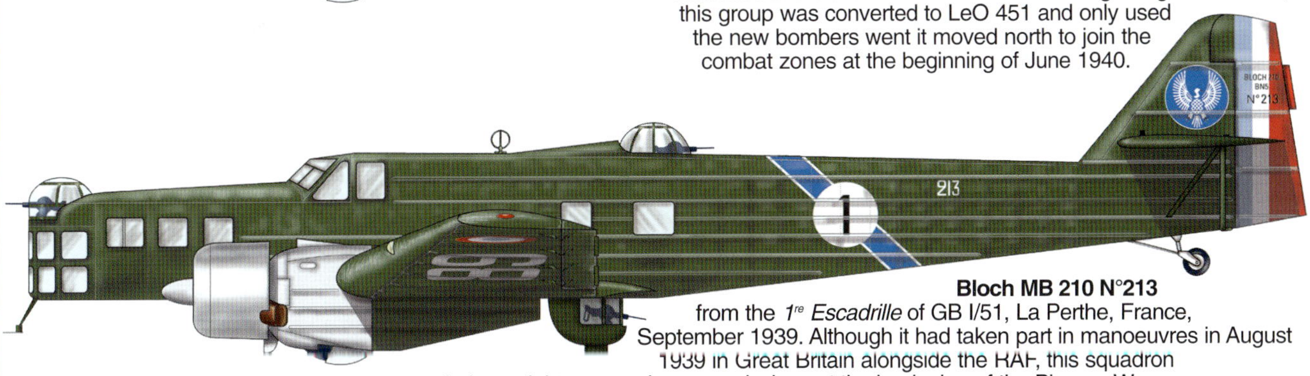

Bloch MB 210 N°213 from the *1re Escadrille* of GB I/51, La Perthe, France, September 1939. Although it had taken part in manoeuvres in August 1939 in Great Britain alongside the RAF, this squadron carried out night reconnaissance missions at the beginning of the Phoney War before being sent to the south of France to convert onto Breguet 691/693s and thus to become GBA I/51. This plane, as its individual number shows, was that of the Flight commander whose particularity was to have his insignia (that of SPA Bi 42, a blue stripe edged with white around the usual place on the fuselage) painted on the tail.

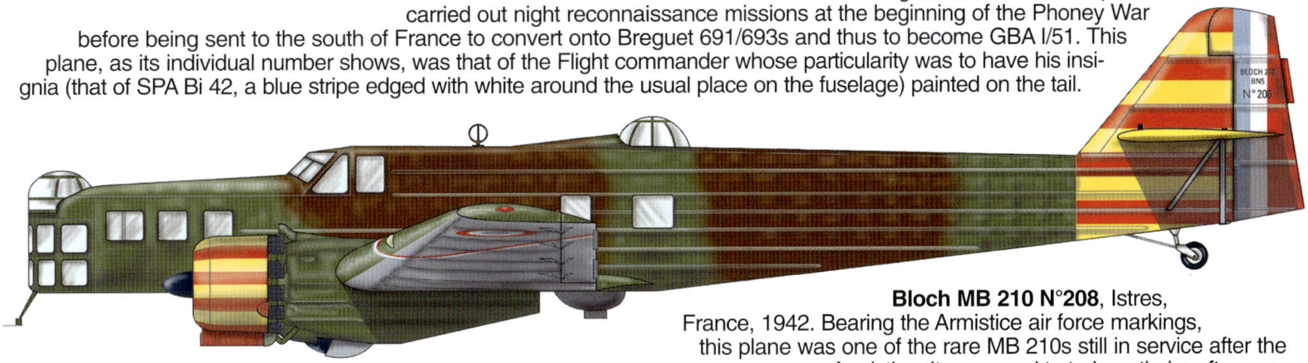

Bloch MB 210 N°208, Istres, France, 1942. Bearing the Armistice air force markings, this plane was one of the rare MB 210s still in service after the Armistice. It was used to train anti-aircraft crews.

Breguet 270

Above:
The Breguet 270 Prototype N°02 seen here in flight shows the machine's peculiar silhouette. This machine which was fitted with two different engines (Hispano-Suiza 12 Hb then Renault 12 Jc) then became the Breguet 271. Its propeller here is fitted with a boss, a rare thing on this machine. *(Coll. V. Gréciet).*

The first flight of the **Breguet 27** took place on 23 February 1929. This two-seat observation sesquiplane (the two wings were of unequal length, unlike the classic biplane) was made entirely of metal. Modifications were carried out several times during the months that followed, especially on the tail.

Apart from this prototype, nine other pre-production series machines were built in order to try out different power plants. Three planes were thus fitted with Renault engines (N°2, 3 and 5); these were **Breguet 271**s; the three others remained at the prototype stage.

Following on the official 1928 programme, a competition for two-seat observation planes (A2) was organised in 1930 in which the Potez 39 among others took part. The planes had to be equipped with a 500 bhp Hispano-Suiza 12 Hb and had to be able to take off in less than 390 feet. Designed to operate from short airstrips, they had to have a wing with a large surface area. The Breguet 27 was declared the winner of the competition and was officially ordered in December 1931. The total number of machines, designated **Breguet 270**, delivered was increased to 140 following two amendments made to the contract in 1932.

The first deliveries were made in December 1932, GO (*Groupe d'Observation*) II/32 becoming the experimental unit for this machine. It was delivered afterwards to GO II/52 and II/55 but the Breguet 270 was almost out-of-date when it entered service; this impression was increased by the fact that the machines it was supposed to replace were scarcely less ancient. In reality the only innovation was their all-metal construction. Apart from this, there were a lot of delays with deliveries, so much so that in the middle of 1935, only a hundred or so were in service in GR I/31, II/31, I/35, II/35 and II/55. A year later, the *35e Escadre* no longer had any Br 270s and the *31e Escadre* used them alongside the ANF-Les Mureaux 117.

The all-metal Breguet had a short operational career since all the planes still in service were handed over to the GARs (*Groupes Aériens de Reserve* – Air Reserve Squadrons) created on 31 December 1937 and some machines were also sent to the testing and instruction centres.

The inventory which was made several days before the beginning of WWII detailed less than a hundred Br 270s available with 19 in the depots. Mobilised in twelve GAO (*Groupes Aériens d'Observation*) in Metropolitan France, they carried out several missions over Germany in the first weeks of the conflict but the heavy losses which these units suffered, equipped as they were with the most vulnerable machines in the air in September 1939, obliged the General Staff to move the units equipped with Potez 390s and Breguet 270s away from the war zone after 6 October. However, because there was nothing to replace them with, the Br 270s stayed in the front line until March 1940 when the Potez 63.11 (which was supposed to succeed them) at last started reaching the units. Thus at the time of the Battle of France (from May 1940 onwards) several GAOs still flew Br 270s alongside the more modern Potez twin-engined machines. The great majority of these aircraft was very quickly lost, abandoned or destroyed by enemy attacks, to such an extent that only 49 of these machines were still present when the stock was officially taken again in July 1940; nearly all of them were scrapped, putting the final touch to the career of this curious bird which neither had success nor the remotest piece of glory.

TECHNICAL SPECIFICATIONS

Type
Two-seat observation plane
Power plant
One Hispano-Suiza 12 Hb liquid-cooled V-12 engine rated at 500 bhp on take-off.
Dimensions
Length: *32 ft 2 in.*
Height: *11 ft 10 in.*
Wingspan: *56 ft 2 in (upper wing), 25 ft (lower wing).*
Total Wing Area: *534.598 sq ft.*
Unladen Weight: *3687 lb.*
Max. Weight: *6 380 lb.*
Performance
Max. Speed: *142 mph at 9900 feet.*
Max. Range: *625 miles.*
Practical Ceiling: *25,575 feet.*
Armament
One 7.5-mm Vickers fuselage-mounted machine gun on the right; twin 7.5-mm Lewis machine guns in rear defensive turret; a bomb launcher in the bay enabling 264 lb of bombs to be carried.

Breguet 270

Breguet 270 N°34 from GAO 518. Bourges, France, 1939. On 10 May 1940, this squadron operating in ZAO Nord zone still had five planes of this type alongside its Potez 63.11. As it can be imagined, the combat missions were given to the Potez aircraft as the Br 270 had long ago shown how vulnerable it was.

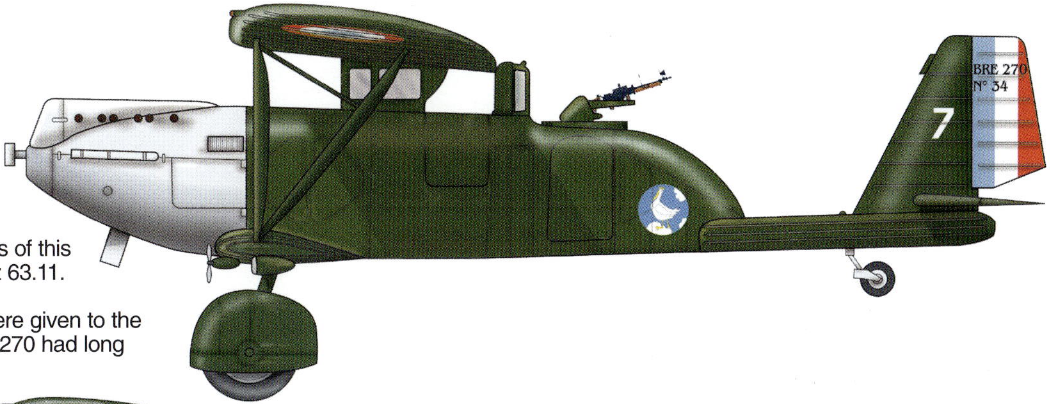

Breguet 270 from GAO 509. Challes-les-Eaux, France, March 1940. This is one of the rare planes of this type to have been camouflaged, which was not superfluous on such a vulnerable machine. The wheel spats have also been removed to prevent mud clogging the wheels.

Breguet 270 from the *Ecole des Observateurs* (Observer School) at Avord, France, spring 1940. Some Br 270s were sent to test and training centres before the beginning of the war, like this one, whose individual number (perhaps its serial number) has been painted in white on the tail fin, as for training aircraft.

Breguet 270 N°57. Tunis el Aouina, Tunisia, July 1940. In May 1940 four Br 270s were inventoried in French North African depots. This one, which is wearing the markings introduced in the summer of 1940, was the last to be retired at the beginning of January 1941. On these planes the serial number was painted on the lower wings and was therefore small.

Breguet 691 to 695

It was in October 1934 that the STAé (the *Service Technique de l'Aéronautique*) launched an official programme for a C3 plane (three-seat fighter) in order to obtain a three-seater armed with a cannon to be used for the interception, escort and fighter director roles. Eight projects, very largely inspired by the studies being carried out in Germany and Holland which eventually produced the Bf 110 or the Fokker G1, answered the tender among which were the Potez 630, the Hanriot 220, the Loire-Nieuport LN 20, the Romano 110 and finally the **Breguet 690**.

This machine was designed by a team led by the engineer Georges Ricard and was distinguishable by a blunt nose, a low cantilever metal wing with fabric-covered ailerons, monocoque Duralumin fuselage which housed the pilot, the navigator and the radio operator-gunner. Armament consisted of two 20-mm Hispano-Suiza cannon in the fuselage, and a single machine gun defending the upper rear sector. It was powered by two Hispano-Suiza 14 Abs developing 680 bhp at 11550 feet and whose propellers rotated in opposite directions in order to reduce the effect of torque. Building on the prototype started in 1935 but an official order for the Breguet 690 was not forthcoming until 26 March 1937, by which time the machine was almost finished and, especially, the Potez 630 had already been selected. This choice meant that the missions the new plane was supposed to carry out had to be redefined; there were further delays (the Hispano-Suiza engines originally intended for Breguet were given to the Potez first) so much so that the prototype only made its first flight on 23 March 1938. Sent to the CEMA the following July, the little twin-engined plane turned out very quickly to be better than the Potez even if its fragile undercarriage meant it had to return to the factory the following month for modifications.

Above: **This photograph of a Breguet 693 from the beginning of the production series (N° 20-29) shows the plane's elegant silhouette and the rear machine gunner's post.** *(SHAA)*

Even before the Breguet 690 N°01 went for trials, an order was placed on 14 June 1938 for a hundred examples of a two-seat aircraft designed especially for the attack and bombing roles, designated **Breguet 691 AB2**; this order was increased to 200 machines a few months later. Changing the original machine was quite simple and consisted of eliminating the third crew member's position and replacing it with a bay able to take eight 110-lb bombs, superimposed on two rows of pylons. Besides, the armament was changed, two 7.5-mm machine guns being installed in the nose, one of them replacing the 20-mm canon which until then was placed on the left side of the cockpit. In order to be better adapted to the Br 691's new missions, all fixed mounted weapons were deflectable downwards by a maximum of 15° which was particularly useful during low-level strafing. Rearward defence consisted of two extra machine guns, one flexible and the other firing downwards through the floor. The nose of the new plane was slightly longer, oil radiators were placed under the engine nacelles and the undercarriage, including the tail wheel, was modified.

The cockpit canopy was now fitted with outward-opening hinged sections and was no longer of the sliding variety. The first 100 Breguet 691s were powered by Hispano-Suiza 14 AB-10/11s developing 700 bhp at Take-off, the next hundred were fitted with HS 14AB-12/13s giving 800 bhp at take-off and which were better suited to the low levels the plane operated at. Finally, apart from the first fifty machines which were equipped with Ratier propellers, the rest had Hamilton Standards.

Production of this twin-engined plane was very rapid, itself an event of some significance in the French aircraft industry of the time, since it was less than a year after the order that the first production series machine appeared - BR 691 N°1 flying on 22 March 1939 and the first production machine on the following 15 May. At the end of August 1939, GBA I/54 the first unit which was to receive this new assault aircraft was transferred to Orléans, with the machines starting to reach the unit during the following October.

Opposite: **The only Breguet 690 prototype, this plane flew for the first time in 1936 and gave rise to the Br 691 to 695 series.** *(DR)*

At the same time, it became clear that the Hispano-Suiza engines were not living up to expectations and the decision was taken to replace them with Gnôme-Rhône 14Ms whose diameter was smaller. Indeed, Br 691 N° 19 was modified to take two GR 14 M-6/7s rated at 700 bhp on take-off and flew for the first time on 29 October 1939 as the **Breguet 693** N°01 before being sent for trials at the CEMA in November. Production of the 691 was therefore stopped with N°78, N°79 becoming Breguet 693 N°1 which flew for the first time on 2 March 1940. From the outside, the plane was identical except for the engines whose cowlings were slightly modified during production, the Br 693s of the 'second' series being given shorter engine cowlings without cooling flaps and flat exhaust pipes which had a slightly propulsive effect which made the aircraft gain a few more mph.

The French authorities realised that national production of engines was not up to meeting demand – a situation which could easily deteriorate further if the industrial potential was destroyed in the case of conflict - decided to call upon foreign engine makers, principally the Americans. With this in mind, the prototype Breguet 690 N°01 was equipped with Pratt and Witney SB4G Twin Wasps, each giving 825 bhp at take off. Installation required some modification since they were lighter; they were also wider than their French counterparts and no longer fitted inside the original cowlings. Fifteen examples from the pre-series were ordered on 27 July 1939 but this figure was increased the following September after war was declared. Modified and called the **Breguet 695**, the new machine took off for the first time on 3 March 1940 but the modifications which had been made both reduced lateral visibility and the plane's performance by about 6%. Despite these failings production was started, flight tests

1. Br 693 N° 109 from GBA I/54 in 1942. '*Sous-Lieutenant De la Porte du Theil*' is written above the 20-mm canon in the fuselage side. The machine guns do not have their round counters. *(SHAA)*

2. Br 691 N°5 coming out of the factory. The plane is simply painted khaki (above) and light grey (below); the upper-side roundels are small.*(DR)*

3. Br 693 N°109 from the *1re Escadrille* of GBA I/54 at the end of 1942. The plane bears the 'white scarves', the last markings of the Vichy Air Force before it was disbanded. *(DR)*

4. Loading 110-lb bombs into a Br 693's bay with glazed doors. The engine air intake is directed towards the outer side of the cowling to correspond to the rotation of the propeller. *(SHAA)*

TECHNICAL SPECIFICATIONS BREGUET 691 (693)

Type

Twin-engined two-seat attack aircraft

Power plants

Two 14-cylinder Hispano-Suiza A4 Ab 10/11 (Gnôme-Rhône 14 M-6/7) air-cooled radial engines developing 670 bhp at take-off (700 bhp).

Dimensions

Length: *31 ft 3 in (31 ft).*
Height: *10 ft 6 in.*
Wingspan: *50 ft 7 in.*
Wing Area: *314.279 sq ft.*
Unladen Weight: *6490 lb (6930 lb).*
Max. Weight: *10593 lb (10670 lb).*

Performance

Max. Speed: *300 mph (296 mph) at 13 200 feet.*
Cruising speed: *254 mph (250 mph) at 13 200 ft.*
Max. Range: *844 miles.*
Max. Ceiling: *28 050 ft.*

Armament

One fixed 20-mm HS 404 canon firing forwards with 60 rounds. Four 7.5-mm MAC 34 machine guns: two firing forward, one for rear defence on a flexible mount and one defending the lower rear sector, firing obliquely through the floor; 880 lb of bombs (8 x 110 lb) carried internally.

One of the most famous Breguet 693s was N° 1013 from *4e Escadrille* of GBA II/54 whose flight insignia, the 'wasp with binoculars' of SPA 259, was surmounted by the nickname '*la Sulfateuse*' (Slang for machine gun). (SHAA)

taking place at the end of April and first deliveries being made to Groupement 18 barely a month later.

As has already been said, production of the Breguet twin-engined assault aircraft was very rapid but these aircraft did not have a significant part to play before the beginning of the Battle of France, which started on 10 May 1940 with the surprise German attack. On that day, 19 Breguet 691s and 38 Br 693 were in the front line.

It was the *1re Escadrille* of GBA I/54 which received the first Breguet 691s, in October 1939. In the following January, the *54e Escadre* formed the *6e Brigade de Bombardement et d'Assaut* with the *51e Escadre*. The planes were very popular with their crews but they did complain about the unreliable engines and fragile landing gear. On 15 April 1940, this brigade was disbanded, *54e Escadre* becoming *Groupement 18* (which regrouped GBA I/54 and II/54 and replaced its Br 691s with 693s) and *51e Escadre* became *Groupement 19* (GBA I/51 and II/51). The first operational sortie of GBA I/54 took place on 12 May over Tongres; seven planes were lost during this mission. At the time, *Groupement 19* was still being converted onto Br 693 in the south of France and only carried out its first operations (alongside the Potez 633 which were very quickly removed) on 20 May. In spite of the difficult conditions under which they flew, these groups scored some successes, especially during dive-bombing attacks started at 3300 feet. They continued up until the Armistice and between them the two *Groupements* carried out 500 sorties, losing more than 100 machines (25 Br 691, 79 Br 693s and two 695s). The machines turned out to be solid, able to take a lot of punishment; they were easy to service (it took barely an hour and a half to change an engine) and were equipped with effective armament. On the other hand as was very much the case with French planes of the time, they were underpowered, particularly at low-level which for a ground-attack aircraft was just not good enough!

Production of these twin-engined aircraft ceased with the Armistice in June 1940. At the time 75 Br 91s, 224 Br 693s and 50 Br 695s had been built and GBA II/35, II/51 and II/54 were disbanded. Only *Groupement 18* was kept, based at Lézignan with a strength of 26 machines regrouping GBA I/51 (to which were assigned the available 695s) and GBA I/54. All the machines still surviving when the Unoccupied Zone was invaded by the Germans were seized. Some were then sent to Italy together with some of the machines which up until then had been mothballed and not assigned to any unit. There they were used for training *Regia Aeronautica* pilots.

As one can imagine, the line of the Breguet 690 gave rise to a certain number of variants and derivatives. Among these, it is worth mentioning the **Breguet 692AB2** which was to have been equipped with Gnôme-Rhône 14Ns but which remained at the project stage since installing these engines called for too many modifications.

The **Breguet 694** was a three-seat reconnaissance plane (the idea of the central position in the original Br 690 being brought back again) and was ordered by Sweden (the order was cancelled in the end), then by Belgium (100 examples of a slightly different version built by SABCA), but it only flew on 20 June 1940 as a prototype which was later given to the Aéronautique Navale. The **Breguet 696B2** was a light two-seat bomber derived from the 693 (with the same engines) with a larger bomb bay and reduced armament; this also flew as a single prototype in November 1939. Series production was planned for the SNAC factory at Bourges but this never happened since 693 production was a priority at the time. The **Breguet 697**N°01 which flew on 19 October 1939 foreshadowed the heavy Br 700 C2 fighter, a French-style *'Zerstörer'*, based on the BR 693 N°17, equipped with 1 070 bhp Gnôme-Rhône 14Ns but of which only a model was made.As for the **Breguet Br 698Bp2** dive-bomber fitted with air brakes, the **Breguet 699 B2** fitted with Pratt and Witney SB4Gs and the **Breguet 810**, the last derivative of the series, a carrier-borne version fitted with all the equipment needed for deck landing (folding wings, air brakes, arrester hooks, etc.) – none of them ever got beyond the drawing board.

Opposite: **Breguet 693 N°65 from *2e Escadrille* of GBA I/51 (the 'rabbit playing the trumpet' of SAL 39 has been painted on the tail) seen at Etampes in May 1940. It is possible that the numbering the aircraft with roman figures was to make believe that new units had appeared.** (SHAA)

Breguet 691 et 693

Breguet Br 691 N°2
(Ser. N°Y-002) from the CEAM at Orléans-Bricy, France, October 1939. This plane took part in the Brussels meeting before the war with a false serial (N° 25) in order to 'disinform'. The Breguet 691 was replaced by the Br 693 on the assembly lines from the 79th example onwards.

Breguet Br 691 N°19 (Ser. N°Y-019) from the 3ᵉ Escadrille of GBA II/54. Vinon, France, April 1940. The 54th wing which became *Groupement d'Assaut* (assault group) N°18 in April 1940, replaced its Br 691s with more powerful Br 693s.

Breguet Br 693 N°93
from the *1re Escadrille* of GBA I/51. Orléans-Bricy, France, June 1940. The SPA Bi 42 stylised Egyptian vulture called the 'reborn phoenix' was worn beforehand by the MB 210s from GB I/51 (cf. Page 55) which was at the origin of the squadron.

Breguet Br 693 N°1 021
from the *2e Escadrille* of GBA I/51. Toulouse-Francazal, France, 25 June 1940. This squadron started the war as GB I/51, equipped with MB 210s and became GBA I/51 after it was converted to Br 693 at the beginning of 1940. Its two flights kept their traditional insignia, here the 'rabbit playing the trumpet' of SAL 39.

Breguet 693

Breguet Br 693 N°84 from the 2e *Escadrille* of GBA I/51. Lézignan-Corbière, France, February 1942. On the Breguets, the white fuselage stripe stopped at the level of the trailing edge of the flaps and was not continued on the nose.

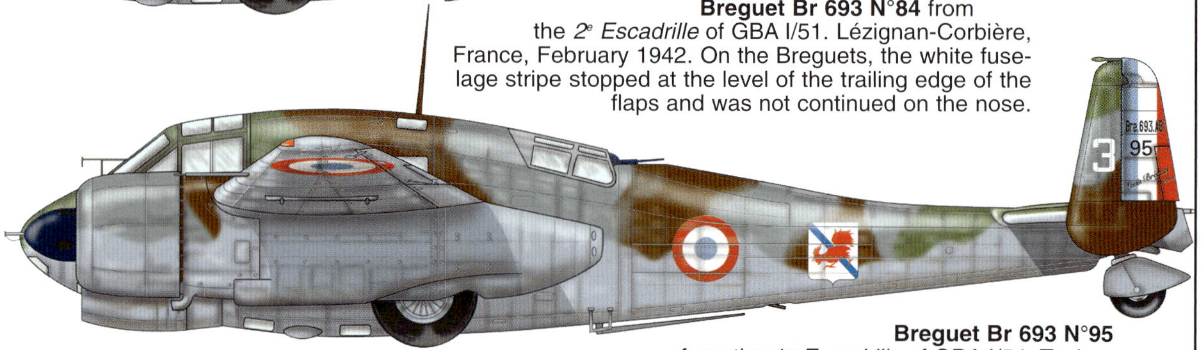

Breguet Br 693 N°95 from the 1re *Escadrille* of GBA I/54. Toulouse-Francazal, France, end of June 1940. On this plane, the engine cowlings are different from the usual ones as they are shorter without flaps but with flat exhaust ejector pipes with a propulsive effect giving a few extra mph. This group was the first to carry out a combat mission, on 12 May 1940 over Tongres.

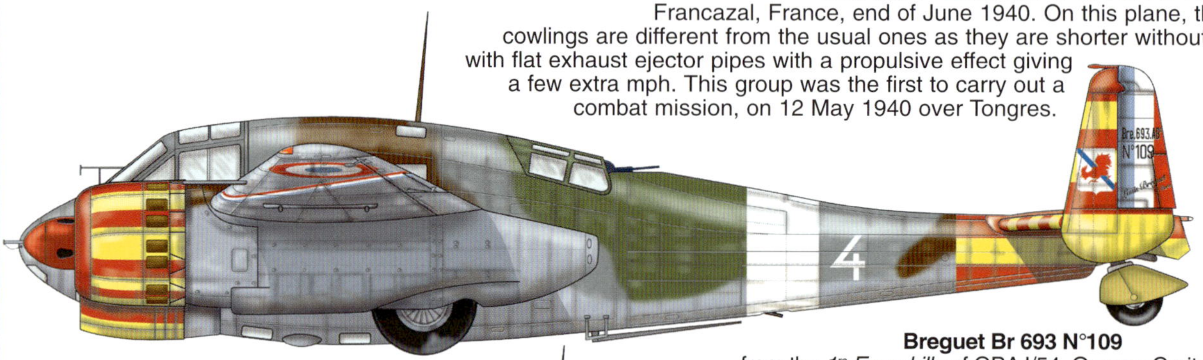

Breguet Br 693 N°109 from the 1re *Escadrille* of GBA I/54. Orange-Caritat, France, November 1942. This plane was christened 'Slt de la Porte du Theil' (under the windshield) after the name of the plane's machine gunner killed in May 1940. It bears the last identification markings introduced a few days before the Armistice Air Force was disbanded.

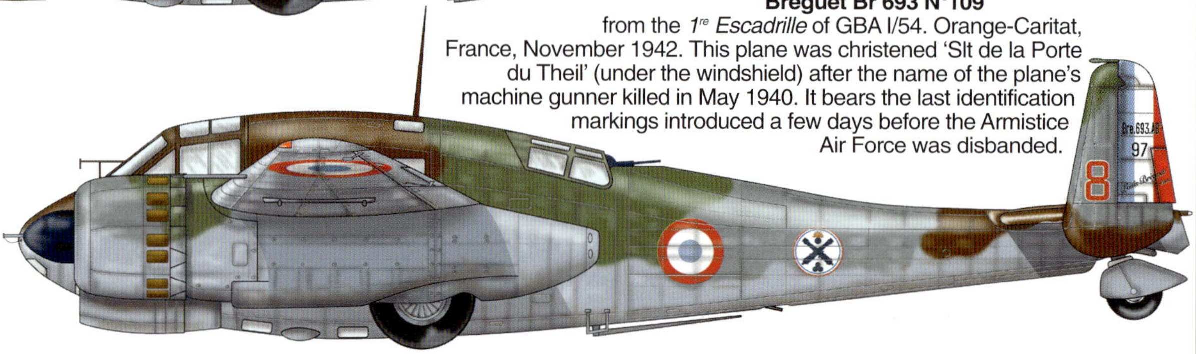

Breguet Br 693 N°97 from the 2e *Escadrille* of GBA I/54. Châteauroux, France, June 1940.

Breguet 693 & 695

Breguet Br 693
N°5 from the
3e Escadrille of GBA II/54. Chartres, France, June 1940. This plane was shot down by four Me 109s on 5 June 1940 as it was attacking armoured columns with four other Br 693s; the crew (Slt Brunet and S/C Martuchet) were killed.

Breguet Br 693 N°1013
from the 4e Escadrille of GBA II/54. Chartres, France, 6 June 1940. Crew: S/C Perrol de Thannberg (pilot) and S/C Badel (machine gunner). The planes from series 1000 did not have Louis Breguet's signature on the tail since they were built by the SNCAN at Bourges and not at Vélizy.

Breguet Br 695 N°4
(unconfirmed) from the *1re Escadrille* of GBA II/54. Landes-de-Bussac, France, June 1940. This is one of the rare examples of this type of plane to have been used operationally during the Battle of France. After the Armistice, all the surviving Br 695s were regrouped within GBA I/51. In the last weeks of fighting, the individual numbers were written in Roman script to make believe that new units were being created.

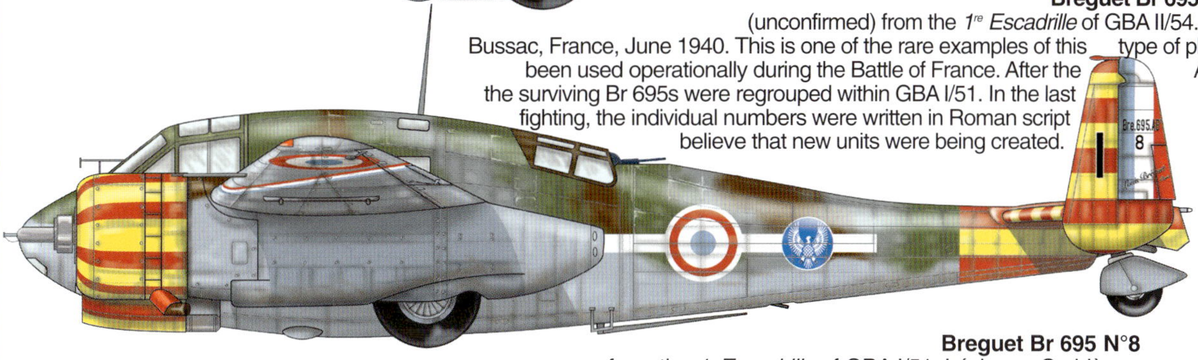

Breguet Br 695 N°8
from the *1reEscadrille* of GBA I/51. Lézignan-Corbières, France, summer 1941.This Breguet belonged to the flight commander, *Capitaine* d'Artemare. After the June 1940 Armistice, only Groupement 18 was kept (GBAs I/51 and I/54).

Caudron CR.714

The Caudron CR. 714 is one of the rare machines designed according to the light fighter concept to have been produced; it has to be said that its career was the reflection of its silhouette, rather slender!

The initial idea of the Caudron engineers was to transform one of their racers which had distinguished themselves in races and other records during the thirties into a warplane; the general idea – together with the very extensive use of wood in the construction - was to enable the aircraft to perform sufficiently well despite the limited power of its engine. In fact, as we will see, nothing came of it and the Armée de l'Air found itself with a machine on its hands which was just as ineffective as it was fragile. It took all the courage and determination of a handful of Polish pilots to give it a bit of prestige.

After being relatively successful in the rapid transport aircraft sector with the Simoun and the Goëland, Caudron took advantage of the lessons learnt with its **C. 690** trainer to propose its **C. 710** for the 'light fighter' category of the 1934 C1 Programme in which the MS 405, among others was also a competitor. This plane was inspired by the racing planes designed by Marcel Riffard which had taken part in the Deutsch de la Meurthe cups in 1934-35 and the prototype first flew on 18 July 1936; but it was turned down, the reason given being the limited power of the engine, a Renault 12 Rol rated at 450 bhp, and in spite of its powerful armament consisting of two 20-mm cannon.

Its successor, the **CR. 713** (**C.711** and **C.712** were racing machines, of which only the second was ever built, flying on 24 December 1936) was designed in the same way and used the fuselage of **CR.710** N° 02. This time however it had retractable undercarriage and a modified tail fin. It was called 'Cyclone' and flew for the first time in December 1937. It was destined for the USSR which finally bought three machines. At the same time Caudron revised the plane's design and started on a new prototype, the Caudron **C.714** which resembled its predecessor but was equipped with a different engine cowling and a triangular tail. It flew for the first time on 6 July 1938 then took part in a series of tests before returning to the factory in October to be fitted with its armament consisting of four 7.5- mm machine guns. It was at that time that the first official orders (20 examples with an option on 180 further machines on 5 November 1938) were placed, with the Armée de l'Air desperately needing to renew its existing fighter pool and the Caudron having the advantage of using an non-priority engine, which at the time was not used to equip the mass-produced fighters like the MS 406 or the D.520. Moreover, the C.714, also nicknamed 'Cyclone', was easy and quick to build, needing in fact only 5 000 man hours, half as much as the MS 406.

The Caudron 714 was built almost entirely from wood except for some of the fairings, made of magnesium; its wing was a one-piece construction with two spars and covered with birch plywood. It was powered by an inverted V-12 Renault engine (the same lay-out as used by the Messerschmitt Bf 109) rated at 450 bhp and armed with four 7.5-mm machine guns paired off in a gondola under each wing.

Although series production started during the summer of 1939, the engine's teething problems caused a lot of delay. Worse, the trials carried out with the first pre-series machine which had been slightly modified (lengthened undercarriage legs, revised tail and air intakes) turned out to be disappointing: the plane now burdened with all its equipment struggled to gain height and its armament was too weak. To cut a long story short, the Armée de l'Air thought the plane inadequate and it decided to halt production sooner than planned with the 90th machine, then supply some to a foreign country (Finland was assigned fifty or so machines), keep some for training and give priority to the Arsenal VG 33 which was

Above: **This CR.714 seen before delivery could be one of the three fighters in the *Patrouille de Guyancourt,* set up on the initiative of the Caudron factory and made up of 'factory' pilots using fighters taken directly off the production lines.** *(Archive WingMasters)*

Opposite: **The Caudron C.690 (here N°8 seen at Toulouse after falling back) was a light plane used by the Armée de l'Air as a fighter trainer. Its general design (wooden construction, Renault engine, cockpit lay-out, shape of the canopy, etc.) recalls its successor, the CR.714, even if the undercarriage is fixed and has wheel spats.** *(Archives WM)*

Above: **Cr 717 N°17 (N° I-207) belonging to *Podporucznik* (Sub-Lieutenant) Aleksy Zukowski, abandoned and captured by the Germans, is without doubt the best-known and most photographed fighter of GC I/145. Note the Polish checkerboard which has replaced the French Roundel on the fuselage.** *(SHAA)*

much more promising. Delivery of the production series machines called the CR.714 C1, was very slow and in March 1940 only nine machines had been received by the Armée de l'Air whereas in the same month five of them reached Finland where they stayed, unused until they were retired from service the following September.

The Armée de l'Air finally found a use for the CR.714s: it gave them to the Polish pilots who had sought refuge in France after the invasion of their country by the Germans. At the beginning of 1940, it was planned to send them to fight against the Russians in Finland in a special unit set up and equipped with CR 714s which were going to be used by the Finns anyway. Although this project fell through, deliveries of the Armée de l'Air's CR.714s had started; they were assigned to the DIAP (*Depot d'Instruction de l'Aviation Polonaise* – Polish Air Force Instruction Depot) and to the GCMP *(Groupe de Chasse et de Marche Polonais)* as training aircraft alongside MS 406s. Faced with the dramatic acceleration in events and the desperate need for fighting units, it was decided to relaunch the original project and get together a fighter squadrons of two flights, GC I/145, sometimes called the Warsaw Polish Fighter Squadron, by giving it the CR 714s to start with while waiting for delivery of the long-overdue MB 152s.

So GC I/145 was created on 2 May 1940 and was at first briefly given the defence of Lyon before being sent to Villacoublay, an aerodrome in the Paris region with the advantage of being very near the Guyancourt factory where the CR 714s were produced. On 19 May there was talk of stopping the whole thing because of the numerous breakdowns, the lack of specialised mechanics and the difficulties encountered simply using this light fighter. However the group was operational on 24 May with about thirty planes on paper and 18 actually operational. They were put at the disposal of ZOA Nord four days later and entrusted with the protection on the Lower Seine valley in particular.

The Poles fought with great courage and determination in spite of inadequate and particularly fragile equipment (for example it was recommended never to over-rev the engine for fear of breaking it which was particularly hard to follow in the heat of the action!) and they scored ten or so kills for the loss of four pilots. On 11 June 1940 as the long-awaited MB 152s were about to be delivered the group only had eleven machines in flying condition left. The pilots finally flew off to Rochefort-sur-Mer and left with other Polish pilots for Great Britain where many of them were back in active service a few weeks later, during the Battle of Britain.

Several variants of the CR 714 were planned which were supposed in their own way to solve the failings of the 714, particularly the underpowered engine and the weak armament. The **CR.715** for example, which came from the 1938 light fighter programme was to have received an Italian Isotta-Fraschini Delta RC-40 engine made under licence by Renault and rated at 300 bhp more than the original motor! This engine was first fitted to a CR 714 airframe and the construction of two other prototypes was started, one of which became the **CR.760** N°01. Unlike the Cyclone, the fuselage was now made of Duralumin even if the wings were still made of wood; the armament was increased to six machine guns. It was test-flown in April 1940 and performed well; it was easy to service with a good weight to performance ratio. It was captured by the Germans and used as a decoy on a dummy airfield.

The second **CR.715** was changed into **CR.770** N°01 after being given a new wing and above all a new engine, an inverted V-16 air-cooled Renault 626 engine fitted with a turbo-charger to replace the original 12Ro1. It took off for the first time in November 1939. Its engine, which had hardly ever been bench tested, broke up in flight. The pilot nonetheless managed to get the thing down in one piece but the trials were never taken up again because in the meantime the CR.760 had turned out to be satisfactory; the CR.770 was stored away in Guyancourt and was probably destroyed in the end to prevent capture.

TECHNICAL SPECIFICATIONS

Type
Single-seat fighter
Power Plant
One V-12 Renault air-cooled 12R03 engine driving a 7 ft 1 in three-blade Ratier propeller
Dimensions
Length: *28 ft 1 in.*
Height: *9 ft 5 in.*
Wingspan: *29 ft 6 in.*
Wing Area: *134.537 sq ft.*
Unladen Weight: *3080 lb.*
Max. Weight: *3850 lb.*
Performance
Max. Speed: *303 mph.*
Range: *562 miles.*
Ceiling: *30,030 ft.*
Armament
Four 7.5-mm MAC M-39 machine guns with 300 rounds each.

Caudron CR.714

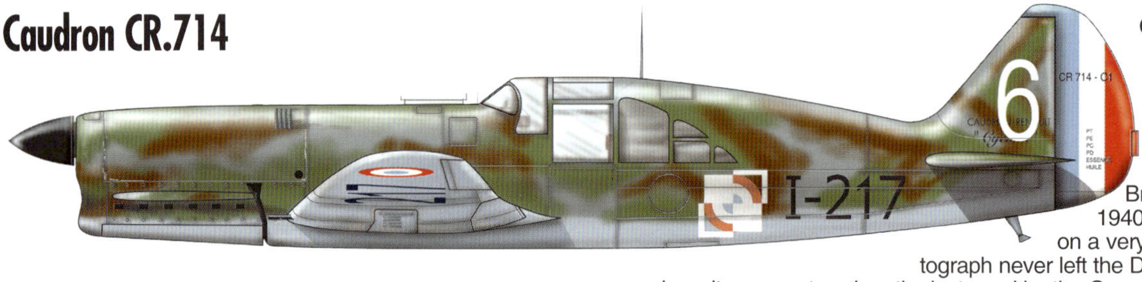

Caudron CR 714 N°27 (Ser. N° I-217) from the DIAP (*Dépôt d'Instruction de l'Aviation Polonaise*). Lyon-Bron, France, June 1940. This plane seen on a very well-known photograph never left the DIAP at Lyon-Bron where it was captured partly destroyed by the Germans.

Caudron CR 714 N°14 (Ser. N°I-204) from the DIAP, Lyon-Bron, France, April 1940. The serial number was painted on the fuselage of the DIAP planes used by the Polish pilots before they were assigned to GC I/145 and sent to fight to the west of Paris, in June 1940.

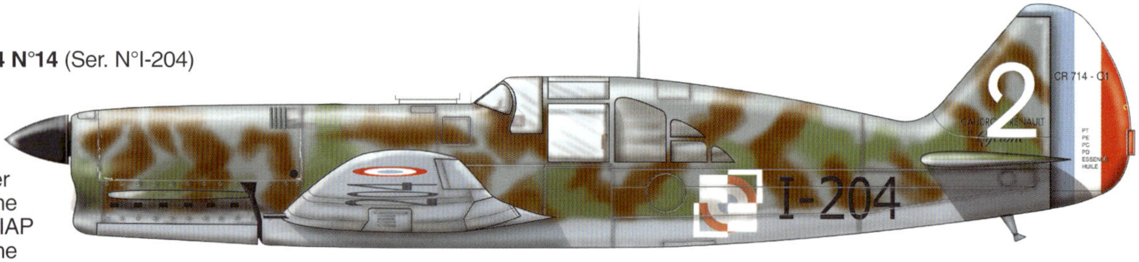

Caudron CR 714 N°10 (Ser. N°I-200) from the 2[e] *Escadrille* of GC I/145. Dreux, France, June 1940. This plane was piloted by *Kapral* (Corporal Andrej Niewara. The planes in the first flight bore their individual numbers on the rudder, those in the second on the fuselage, as here.

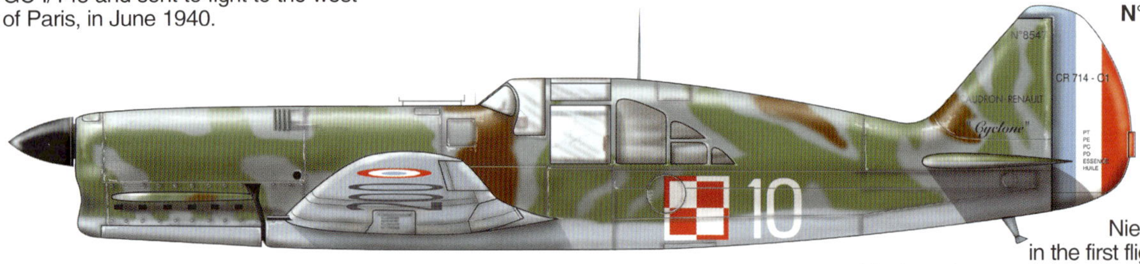

Caudron CR 714 N°18 (Ser. N°I-208) from the 1re *Escadrille* of GC I/145. Dreux, France, June 1940. Flown by *Podporucnik* (Sub-Lieutenant) Marian Lukaszewicz, this plane made a forced landing on the Dreux airfield on 8 June 1940. GC I/145 was the only unit entirely made up of Polish pilots in the Armée de l'Air during the Battle of France. Its planes bore the Polish checkerboard, replacing the fuselage roundel.

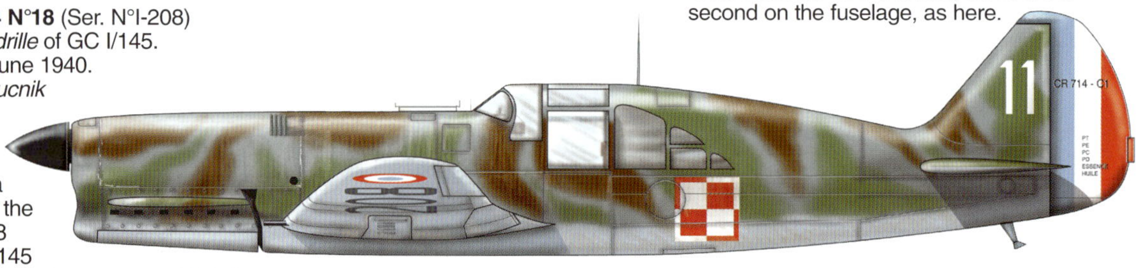

Caudron CR 714 N°17 (Ser. N°I-207) from the 1[re] *Escadrille* of GC I/145, Dreux, France, June 1940. This plane flown by *Podporucznik* (Sub-Lieutenant Aleksy Zukowski made a forced landing when returning from a mission.

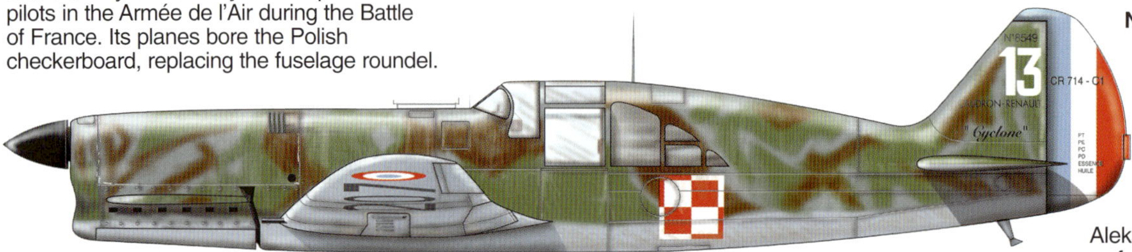

Curtiss H-75A-1 to A-4

In order to take part in the competition in May 1935 announced by the USAAC (United States Army Air Corps), the future USAF, in order to find a replacement for the Boeing P-26 'Peashooter', the Curtiss-Wright Company decided to produce an all-metal low-wing monoplane fighter privately in October 1934. It had a monocoque fuselage and retractable undercarriage and the company's own designation 'Model 75'. The project was given to a team led by its chief engineer, Donovan 'Don' Berlin.

As no other competitor was ready on the set date and as the Wright engine originally planned was thought to be unsatisfactory, it was first with a 700 bhp Pratt and Witney R-1535 Twin Wasp Junior radial engine, then with a single row XR 1820 engine that the Curtiss prototype now designated Model 75B took part in the competition in August 1935 then in April 1936, coming second behind the Seversky SEV-1XP (the future P-35). The Seversky won and a production series was ordered. At the time these two planes were the first two modern American fighters with enclosed cockpit and retractable undercarriage, the Curtiss aircraft featuring a special retracting system where the leg turned through 90° and the wheel came up into the well, flush with wing.

Despite this failure, the Curtiss prototype had shown undeniable qualities and a contract was signed in July 1936 with the American Government for the building of three prototypes, first designated Y1P-36 then finally **P-36**, and powered by a Pratt and Witney R-1830-13 Twin Wasp radial engine; the cockpit had been improved and the tail wheel was now retractable also. Trials carried out in the summer of 1937 with these machines proved to be very encouraging and it was decided to mass-produce them, 200 examples being therefore ordered in July 1937. They were modified a little, with a different propeller and a slightly more powerful engine. The first of the 178 **P-36A**s was supplied to the USAAC in April 1938. For the USAAC this was the biggest contract ever placed for a fighter. During the whole production period for this version which ceased in June 1939, a number of modifications (more than 80!) were made to the original aircraft which meant the machine ended up being heavier and therefore slower. A P-36A powered by a 1000 bhp P & W R-1830-25 engine gave rise to the **P-36B**, the fastest of them all. The last 31 examples were fitted

Above: **Curtiss H-75 A-1 from the 1[re] *Escadrille* of GC I/4. The single machine gun in each leading edge which was a feature of this version is clearly visible here.** *(SHAA)*

Below: **Curtiss H-75 A-1 N°35 from the 3[e] Escadrille of GC II/5. The Sioux's head is visible on the fuselage on which the roundel has not yet been painted. Note the very special camouflage scheme with large patches, as well as the little roundels, about a foot across, on the underside.** *(Collection J. Delmas)*

Above: **The way in which the lower colour (light grey-blue) stretches over the engine cowling of this H-75 A-1 from the 'Sioux' (GC II/5, 3^e^ *Escadrille*) photographed during the Battle of France is rather unusual. The undercarriage of the Curtiss and its variants including the P-40 pivoted through 90° when retracted to come up into the wheel well, flush with the wing.** *(SHAA)*

with a 1 200 bhp engine and re-designated **P-36C**. Finally, the 10th P-36A, fitted with a completely new engine and extensively modified, became the P-40.

The 'Model 75' was only moderately successful in its country of origin; this was because it was much more successful abroad which was where it won its laurels. Realising that national outlets for its fighter were rather restricted, the Curtiss Co. quickly decided to sell it on the export market as the '**Hawk 75**', a name which recalled one of the company's earlier foreign successes, the Curtiss Hawk III. Two prototypes powered by a 9-cylinder Wright Cyclone GR-1820-G3 radial engine were therefore built at the same time as the Y1P-36 prototypes. These machines were identical except for their armament, one having only one 12.7-mm machine gun and another 7.62-mm one in the engine cowling; the other was fitted with two extra ones in the wings. Designated **Hawk 75-H** and mass-produced, these planes were sold to China, Argentina and Thailand, among others.

But it was above all the Armée de l'Air which became one of Curtiss's main export customers and which enabled it to win its biggest successes in aerial combat.

At the end of 1937, the *Conseil Supérieur de l'Air* (the Air Council) realised that French aircraft manufacturers alone could not equip the Armée de l'Air with enough fighters, especially as the targets of Plan V, the one in effect at the time, seemed to be totally unattainable. It therefore decided to call upon foreign manufacturers. Several missions were decided upon and sent off, including one to the URSS, but with the exception of the Netherlands, from which fifty or so Koolhoven FK 58 fighters were purchased, no other European country seemed capable of supplying the desired equipment in sufficient quantities. Turning very logically to the United States, where unofficial negotiations had been under way since the end of 1937 by Baron de la Grange, a friend of President Roosevelt, the newly-appointed Air Minister, Guy la Chambre, gave instructions for several hundred foreign, modern fighters to be purchased. Because of the French demands, especially for very short delivery dates, the choice was limited to two machines with very similar performances: the Seversky P-35 and the Curtiss H-75/P-36. The USAAC having chosen the Seversky, the French turned therefore to its unlucky competitor, the Curtiss.

Discussions were particularly long and difficult, the French complaining that the unit purchase price was much higher than that of a MS 406 or a MB 152. The delays suffered by French national aircraft production as well as the deterioration in the European political situation meant that all obstacles were eventually removed and a first contract for a hundred machines, called the **H-75A-1** (for Curtiss, the suffix A identified export models equipped with retractable undercarriage) was finally signed in May 1938. These planes were identical to their P-36A counterparts ordered by the USAAC and which were beginning to come off the production lines; they were powered by 1 050 bhp Pratt and Witney Twin Wasp R-1830 SC3G radials and fitted with French equipment (sights, radio, etc.). The throttle was reversed to comply with general practice within the Armée de l'Air and the various instruments were calibrated according to the metric system. Finally the armament chosen consisted of four 7.5-mm Browning machine guns (two on the engine cowling and two in the wings) built under licence in France.

Tested at Buffalo in the USA in November 1938 by one of the Curtiss pilots, the first plane intended for France was then tested by one of the CEMA delegation members at the trials. The machines were dismantled, crated and shipped to France by boat to le Havre, where they arrived on 24 December before being sent to the SNCAC *(Société Nationale de Construction Aéronautique du Centre)* at Bourges which was given the job of re-assembling them; this started at the beginning of 1939.

The international situation got worse and worse especially after the Munich Crisis (September 1938) and French aircraft manufacturers were still apparently unable to meet the targets already set. Further negotiations were therefore held to purchase the new Curtiss fighter, the H-81 (P-40), which was equipped with an Allison in-line engine. Unfortunately this project came to nothing because of delays in producing this new power unit. So the French fell back on a slightly improved version of the H-75, a possible alternative which had already been envisaged when the first contract was signed.

This time the plane, with a reinforced rear fuselage, was equipped with a Twin Wasp SG3G radial - slightly more powerful than its predecessor - and, from N°141 onwards, was armed with two extra machine guns in the wings (the modification was carried out later on certain examples). These new machines, of which a further 100 were ordered in 1939 (and numbered from N°101 onwards) were designated **H-75A-2**.

A group of GC I/4 Curtiss H-75s in flight. The first plane (A-1 N°99) flown by Sergent Lemare bears the 'Egyptian lammergeyer' of the 2e *Escadrille* (SPA 153) under the windshield and the black and white 'mourning' stripes at the base of the tail. *(Archives WM)*

In September 1939, at the beginning of the conflict, all the fighters had been delivered to France and taken on charge by the Armée de l'Air. The first units to receive the new Curtiss were GCs I/5, II/5 and I/4 in March/April 1939. These squadrons were still equipped with D.500/501s during their conversion period; in theory they should have received the new Bloch 151s and 152s but their entry into service was being delayed. These units were re-equipped and were followed by GC II/4 which received its new machines in at the beginning of the summer of 1939.

In the following August a new French mission was sent to the United States with the task of purchasing extra fighters as national production still could not catch up on the Plan V objectives which apparently could not be met before the following spring.

After difficult negotiations brought about by the recent declaration of neutrality announced by the USA now confronted with France as one of the warring parties, and in spite of a price increase, a contract was signed at the beginning of October not only for 535 H-75s, deliveries to be spread out over one year, but also for a hundred of the new, and at last available, H-81s. Moreover, 1 000 engines and propellers were also ordered and in the long term, the Twin Wasp engine was even to be made by Talbot under licence in France.

The first aircraft from the new contract reached France in March 1940 and slightly more than a hundred of these machines (designated **H-75A-3**), equipped with the more powerful 1200 bhp Pratt and Witney R-1830 Twin Wasp SIC3G engine (the numbers followed on those of the preceding aircraft, starting at 201) were received by the Armée de l'Air before the hostilities ceased. At the time several dozens of H-75s were still at sea: some were lost when their transport sank, others (those aboard the *Béarn* or the *Jeanne d'Arc*) were stocked in Antigua; thirty or so were unloaded at Casablanca in Morocco. The **H-75 A-4**, officially called the H-751, differed from its predecessors in that it had a 1 200 bhp (at take-off) Wright Cyclone R-1820-G205A engine and needed a different shape of engine cowling; it was never used in combat even though it had been ordered in large numbers and only a few examples ever reached France before the Armistice.

At the beginning of the war four fighter squadrons were equipped with the Curtiss fighter, GC I/4 and II/4, and GC I/5 and II/5. All were based at Rheims and were very rapidly deployed on their 'war fields' located respectively at Wez-Thuizy, Xaffevilliers, Suippes and Toul-Croix-de-Metz. The results of the Curtiss during the Phoney War were more than honourable since they totalled 42 kills with 22 probables for the loss of 'only' five pilots and 18 aircraft. Although it was liked by the pilots, especially for its comfort, it was not without failings, the most important of which were its lack of power compared with most modern enemy aircraft, its insufficient armament (particularly those equipped with only four machine guns) and its inadequate protection (especially for the fuel tanks).

During the Battle of France, all the H-75s were committed all the time; a fifth squadron, GC III/2 which beforehand flew MS 406s, was re-equipped at the very end of May. At first they were sent into Belgium to support the ground forces during the initial offensive; then after 10 June, they were chased from one base to another by the irresistible German onslaught. On about 20 June, all the surviving planes started to fall back on French North Africa and therefore crossed the Mediterranean under their own steam. The score at the end of the fighting was in favour of the Curtiss-equipped units which accounted for more than 300 enemy aircraft (233 confirmed and 84 probables) for the loss of thirty or so pilots in combat and through accidents. A number got their Ace's title flying this machine (Edmond Marin la Meslée, the 'Ace of Aces' with 16 confirmed kills, Camille Plubeau and even Jean Accart), the first flight of GC I/5 getting five of its pilots onto the list of French aces for 1939-1940. On the other hand, the material losses were a lot less glorious. It is estimated (although the exact figures remain unknown) that about a hundred machines were lost for various reasons (combat, accident, destruction on the ground, etc.), about a third of the total number of machines which were delivered.

After the Armistice, on 20 July 1940, 231 Curtiss H-75s of all variants were inventoried; one lot (45 machines) remained in Metropolitan France and the rest, the majority, found themselves in North Africa

TECHNICAL SPECIFICATIONS

Type
Single-seat fighter

Power plant
One 14-cylinder Pratt and Witney double row radial engine rated at 1 050 bhp (A-1 and A-2) and 1 200 bhp (A-3) on take-off, and driving a Curtiss-Electric 10-foot diameter three-blade propeller.

Dimensions
Length: *29 feet.*
Height: *8 ft 11 in.*
Wingspan: *37 ft 6 in.*
Wing Area: *235.924 sq ft.*
Weight empty: *4703 lb.*
Max. Weight: *5896 lb (A-2: 5975 lb)*

Performance
Max. Speed: *304 mph (A-2: 312 mph)*
Max. Range: *918 miles.*
Practical Ceiling: *33 000 feet*

Armament
Two 7.5-mm FN-Browning machine guns on the engine cowling, two others (A-1) or four others (A-2 and A-3) in the wings.

Opposite:
the H-75 A-2 N°183 belonging to *Lieutenant-Colonel* Haegelen, the WWI ace, bore the flying stork insignia of SPA 103 on the rear of the fuselage, in a non-regulation way. At the time this shot was taken (1939), the roundel had not yet been painted on the fuselage. When this WWI ace, a test pilot for Hanriot (SNCAC) headed the ELD at Bourges made up of Polish pilots, the red and white checkerboard was added on the tail. *(SHAA)*

Below:
Curtiss H-75 A-2 N°104 from GC I/5 at the beginning of the war, without insignia or fuselage roundel. *(Archives WingMasters)*

(186 aircraft, of which about a hundred in Morocco) where all the squadrons equipped with this fighter had rallied just before hostilities ceased. The three Curtiss units which were finally allowed to remain active were stationed at Dakar (GC I/4), in the Senegal, at the time *Afrique Occidentale Française* (AOF - French West Africa), Rabat (GC I/5) and Casablanca (GC II/5) in Morocco; GCs II/2 and II/4 were disbanded in August 1940.

During the two years which followed the end of hostilities with Germany, these squadrons had to face serious moral crises during which they had to fight against, among others, British troops. This was true of the attack on the fleet at Mers-el-Kébir when GC I/5 and II/5 succeeded in getting their planes airworthy again (they had been put out of action following the Armistice) in order to try and oppose Fleet Air Arm aircraft. These two squadrons also protected the bombers participating in the reprisal raid on the British base at Gibraltar, following the show of strength at Dakar during which GCI/4 had also been made to intervene. Their last intervention was during Operation 'Torch', the allied landings in Morocco (November 1942), when the H-75s from GC I/5 and II/5 fought against Fleet Air Arm and US Navy Air Force planes.

These combats marked the beginning of the end of the French Curtisses which were now out-of-date and getting more and more difficult to service and keep airworthy because of the lack of spare parts. At the end of 1941, it was planned to replace the H-75s serving in Africa with D. 520s which were to have been the 'standard' fighters of the Armée de l'Air. As priority was given to the units still equipped with MS 406s and MB 152s, only the second flight of GC II/5 had been converted to the D.520 when, in November 1942, the Vichy air Force ceased to exist. According to the plan, this conversion was to have been finished in 1943. Sweden declared an interest in some of the remaining 76 examples (out of a total strength of 129) still in service in the fighter groups. After the troops in North Africa rallied the Allied cause, the surviving Curtisses (including the A-4s with the Wright engine) were assigned to training and liaison missions. The machines which managed to survive the war were used by the training centre at Cazaux where they reamined in service until July 1949 at which date they were definitively retired from service.

Curtiss H-75 A-2 N° 140 from the 3^e^ *Escadrille* of GC II/5 bearing the famous 'Sioux's Head', the emblem inherited from the Lafayette Flight, made up of American volunteers during the Great War, and painted on a green diagonal stripe. Note the figure 1 painted on the right wing. *(SHAA)*

Curtiss H-75

Curtiss H-75 A-2 N°105 (Ser. N° U-005) from the *1re Escadrille* of GC I/4. Wez-Thuizy, France, September 1939. Pilot: *Capitaine* Patrick O'Byrne, commanding officer of the 1st Flight. All the planes in the *4e Escadre* had a 'mourning' stripe at the base of the tail in honour of Capitaine Bonneton, who died in 1922. This practice lasted until the arrival of the P-39.

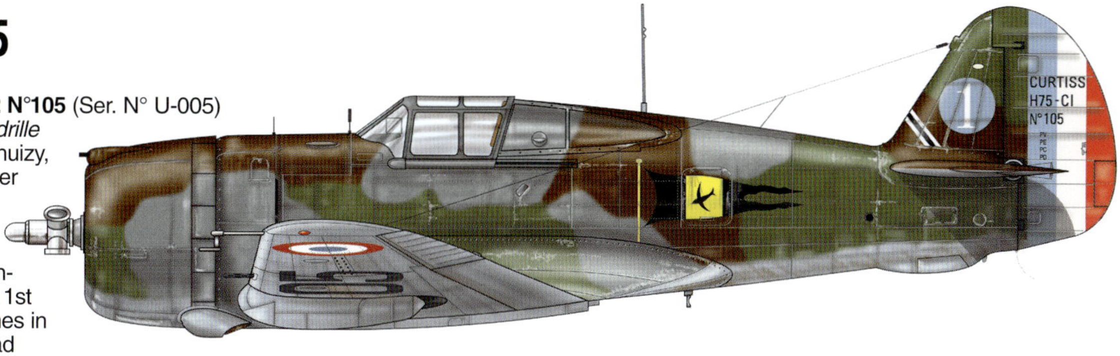

Curtiss H-75 A-1 N°48 (Ser. N° X-847) from the *1re Escadrille* of GC I/4. Wez-Thuizy, France, April 1940. The unit insignia were theoretically forbidden when the fuselage roundel was introduced and the emblems were moved under the cockpit in this unit in order to get round this rule which was never really applied anyway.

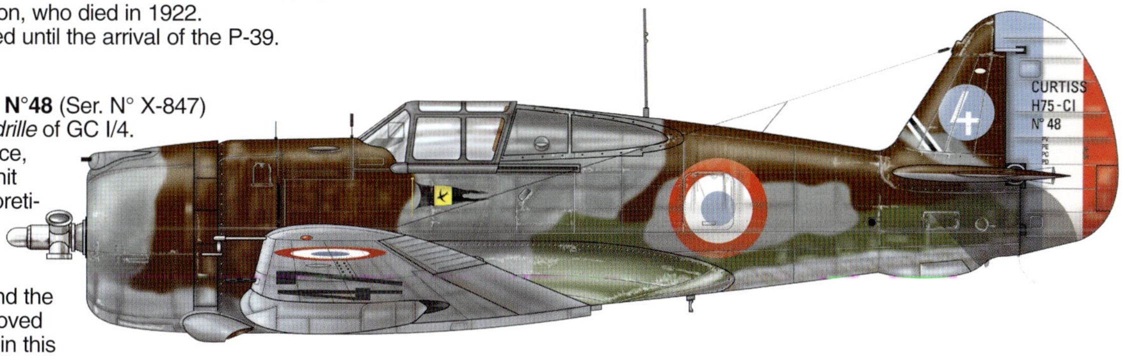

Curtiss H-75 A-1 N°84 (Ser. N° X-883) from the *1re Escadrille* of GC I/4. Dunkerque-Mardyk, France, beginning of May 1940. This plane made a forced landing on its airfield on 17 May. It was equipped with four wing-mounted machine guns and was abandoned after being sabotaged.

Curtiss H-75 A-3 N°301 from the *2e Escadrille* of GC I/4. Dakar-Ouakam, Senegal, end of 1940. This group was sent to French West Africa in July 1940 because of the British threat to the region: indeed on 8 July, the Cruiser '*Richelieu*' was torpedoed in the port at Dakar by a Swordfish. The stripe on the tail was blue in the 1st Flight and red in the 2nd.

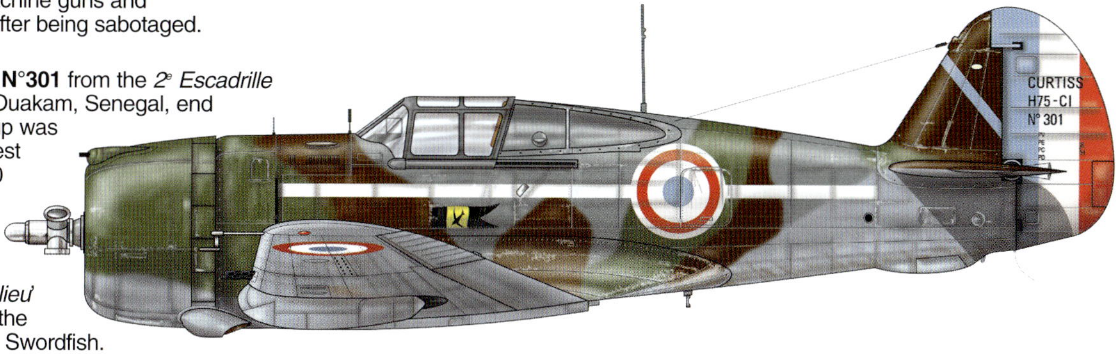

Curtiss H-75

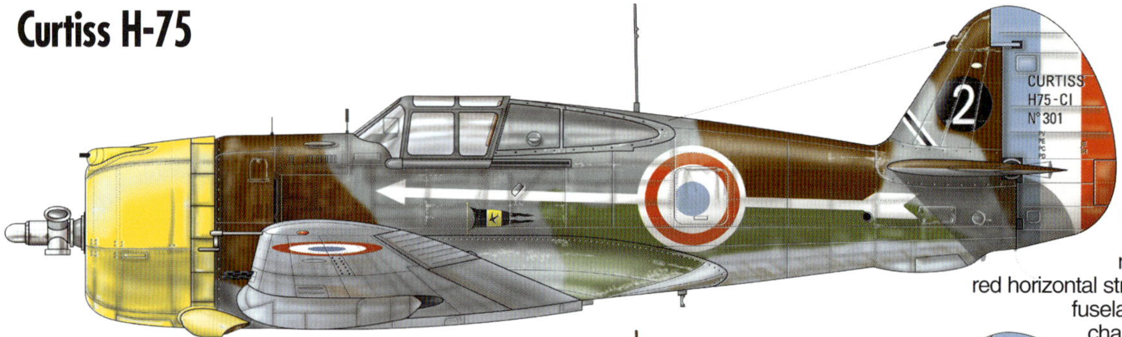

Curtiss H-75 A-3 N°301 from the *1re Escadrille* of GC I/4. Dakar-Ouakam, Senegal, 1941. On this plane only the engine cowling has been painted yellow and has not yet received the red horizontal stripes, and the white fuselage stripe has been changed into an arrow.

Curtiss H-75 A-3 N°275 from the *1re Escadrille* of GC I/4. Dakar-Ouakam, Senegal, 1942. Taking advantage of the fact that the roundel and fuselage stripe had to disappear, the ground staff have camouflaged this machine in a most unusual way with a grey wavy line running along the whole flank.

Curtiss H-75 A-2 N°187 from the *1re Escadrille* of GC I/4. Dakar-Ouakam, Senegal, August 1942. Pilot: S/C Debethune. With the appearance of the tricolour stripes on the wings, the code normally painted on the underside of H-75 A-1s and A-2s disappeared.

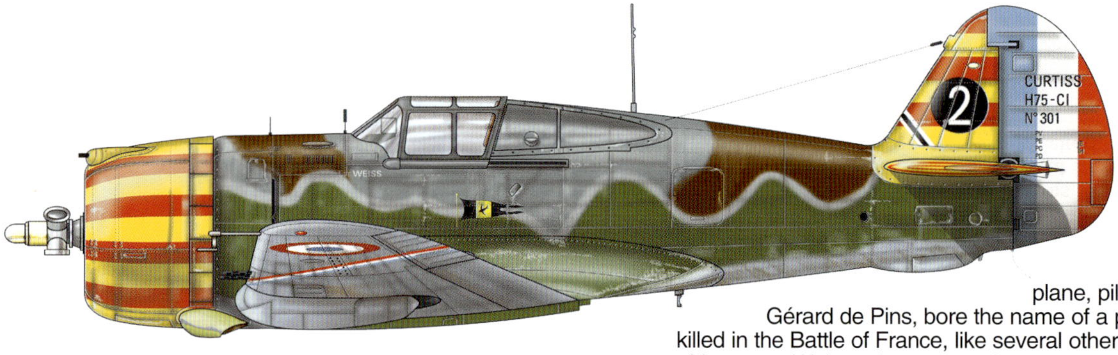

Curtiss H-75 A-3 N°301 from the *1re Escadrille* of GC I/4. Dakar-Ouakam, Senegal, 1942. Partly repainted in rather an original manner this plane, piloted by *Lieutenant* Gérard de Pins, bore the name of a pilot who had been killed in the Battle of France, like several other planes in this unit. *Lieutenant* Weiss, whose name is painted under the windshield, was shot down in June 1940.

Curtiss H-75

Curtiss H-75 A-1 N°85 (Ser. N° X-884) from the *2e Escadrille* of GC I/4. Rheims, France, July 1939. The pilot of this plane, S/C Joannès Cucumel, with 8 confirmed kills in 1939-40, was killed in a training flight in August 1942.

Curtiss H-75 A-1 N°79 (Ser. N° X-878) from the 2e Escadrille of GC I/4. Dakar-Ouakam, Senegal, January 1941. Pilot: A/C Pierre Feuillat. The fuselage roundel is a strange size as is the shape of the front of the white identification stripe on which the flight insignia has been painted.

Curtiss H-75 A-3 N°295 from the *2e Escadrille* of GC I/4. Dakar-Ouakam, Senegal, 1942. This plane whose number has been painted under the windshield was flown by *Sergent* Georges Lemare, who at the time had 5 kills to his credit and who completed his tally under less favourable climes in the 'Normandie-Niemen' Regiment in Russia.

Curtiss H-75 A-3 N°279 from the *3e Escadrille* of GC II/4. Nancy-Azelot, France, April 1940. Nicknamed '*Fan-Fan la Tulipe*', this plane was flown by S/C Antoine Casenobe, with 7 confirmed kills to his credit during the Battle of France.

Curtiss H-75

Curtiss H-75 A-2 N°101 (Ser. N° U-001) from the *3e Escadrille* of GC II/4. Xaffevilliers, France, beginning of May 1940. In spite of there being a roundel on the fuselage, the large unit insignia (the red devil of SPA 160) has been kept on the fuselage.

Curtiss H-75 A-1 N°67 (Ser. N° X-866) from the *4e Escadrille* of GC II/4. Rheims-Courcy, France, July 1939. Pilot: *Adjudant* Villey. The 4th and 5th fighter wings, both equipped with Curtisses, were based at Rheims until mobilised in August 1939.

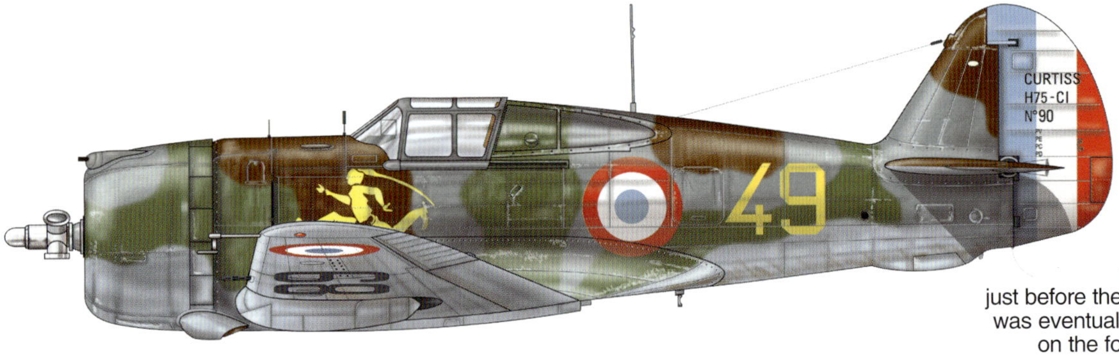

Curtiss H-75 A-1 N°90 (Ser. N° X-889) from the *4e Escadrille* of GC II/4. Meknes, Morocco, end of June 1940. Having crossed the Mediterranean just before the Armistice, GC II/4 was eventually disbanded there on the following 25 August.

Curtiss H-75 A-1 N°14 (Ser. N° X-843) from GC I/5. Suippes, France, November 1939. This H-75, the plane flown by *Commandant* Murtin of the Group's Headquarters, bears a blazon incorporating the insignia of the two flights of GC I/5 (the stork of SPA 67 and the falcon of SPA 75).

Curtiss H-75

Curtiss H-75 A-1 N°49 (Ser. N° X-848) from the *1re Escadrille* of GC I/5. Suippes, France, September 1939. Pilot *Capitaine* Jean Accart, commanding the 1st Flight and one of the French Curtiss aces with 12 confirmed kills and four probables.

Curtiss H-75 A-2 N°158 (Ser. N° U-058) from the *1re Escadrille* of GC I/5. Suippes, France, May 1940. This is one of the planes used by *Lieutenant* Edmond Marin la Meslée, the ace of aces of the Battle of France with 16 confirmed kills and 4 probables, all obtained before 10 June 1940. He was killed in action in February 1945 aboard a P-47 from GC I/5 which in the meantime had become 'Champagne'.

Curtiss H-75 A-2 N°224 from the *1re Escadrille* of GC I/5. Rabat, Morocco, beginning of 1942. In GC I/5 the planes with the codes '2' and '3' were assigned to the patrol commanders in the flights. *Lieutenant* Briant in turn was given this role as the figure painted on an orange disk (characteristic of the 1st Flight) shows.

Curtiss H-75 A-1 N°14 (Ser. N° X-813) from the *2e Escadrille* of GC I/5. Suippes, France, October 1939. The individual number has not yet been painted inside the coloured disk which however is already on the tail.

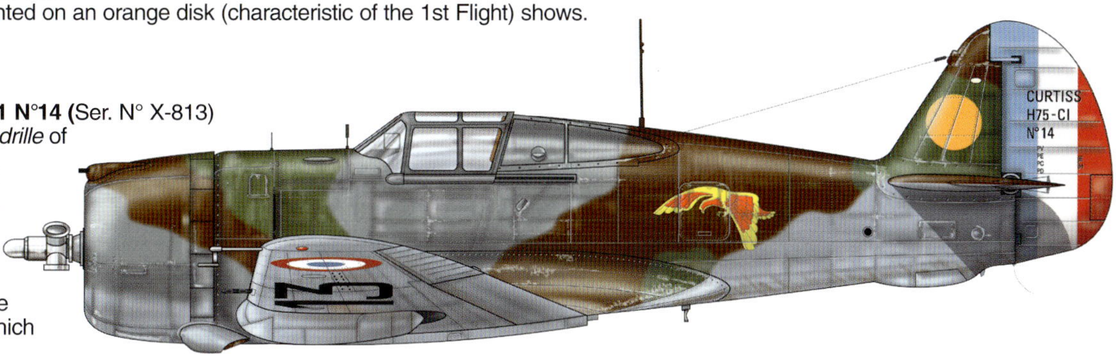

Curtiss H-75

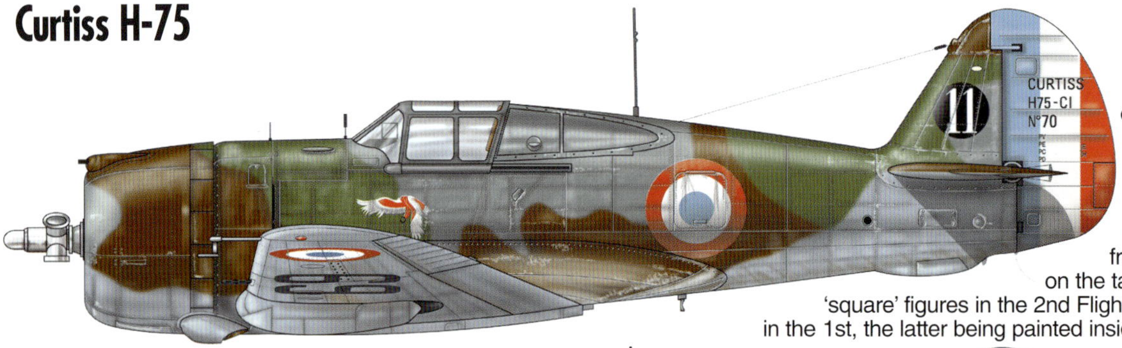

Curtiss H-75 A-1 N°70 (Ser. N° X-869) from the *2e Escadrille* of GC I/5. Suippes, France, beginning of 1940. Before the Armistice the individual number on planes from GC I/5 painted on the tail was made up of 'square' figures in the 2nd Flight and 'Cyrillic-style' in the 1st, the latter being painted inside an orange disk.

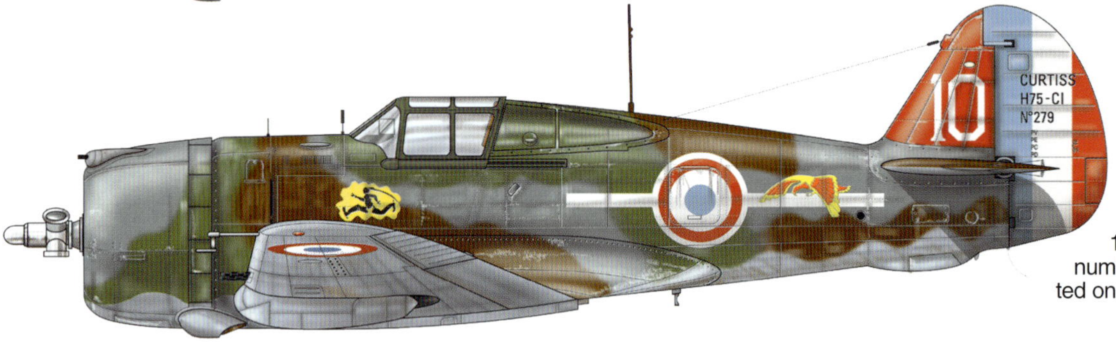

Curtiss H-75 A-3 N°279 from the *2e Escadrille* of GC I/5. Rabat, Morocco, end of 1940. The individual number has been painted on a red background.

Curtiss H-75 A-3 N°267 from the *2e Escadrille* of GC I/5. Rabat, Morocco, 1940. This plane belongs to *Sous-Lieutenant* Camille Plubeau, one of the aces from the Battle of France with 14 confirmed kills and four probables. According to a widespread habit in this unit, the individual number was made up of the last two figures of the serial number.

Curtiss H-75 A-2 N°193 (Ser. N° U-092) from the *2e Escadrille* of GC I/5. Rabat, Morocco, 1941. Pilot: Lt Max Vincotte. GC II/4 was disbanded in August 1940 and its former pilots were allowed to keep the insignia of their previous flight in this group: here the 'Tom Thumb' of SPA 155 as well as the SPA 75's 'vulture'.

Curtiss H-75

Curtiss H-75 A-1 N°88 from the *2e Escadrille* of GC I/5. Rabat, Morocco, November 942. This plane, which bears the insignia of SPA 155 under the cockpit, was seriously damaged during the brief but violent fighting during Operation 'Torch', the Allied landings in French North Africa.

Curtiss H-75 A-1 N°35 (Ser. N° X-834) from the *3e Escadrille* of GC II/5. Toul-Croix-de-Metz, France, November 1939. Pilot: *Adjudant* Jean Dugougeon. On this plane, the large patches of camouflage were typical of the first production series machines; the unit insignia (the Sioux's Head inherited from the famous *Escadrille Lafayette* of WWI) has been painted on a diagonal green stripe, characteristic of the 3rd flight.

Curtiss H-75 A-3 N°214 from the *1re Escadrille* of GC II/5. Casablanca, Morocco, 1941. This plane of which the bottom of the fuselage has been repainted. bears no unit insignia. Note that the '*matricule militaire*' (serial number) was no longer painted on the H-75 A-3s, like this one.

Curtiss H-75 A-2 N°154 from the *3e Escadrille* of GC II/5. Casablanca, Morocco, 1942. This plane has been partly repainted in order to cover the white stripe and the roundel which were on the fuselage, as imposed by the official directive of the winter of 1941-42.

Curtiss H-75

Curtiss H-75 A-1 N°2 (Ser. N° X-801) from the *4e Escadrille* of GC II/5, Rheims, France, May 1939. Pilot: *Sergent* Jean Gisclon.

Curtiss H-75 A-3 N°296 from the *4e Escadrille* of GC II/5. St-Denis-du-Sig, Algeria, July 1940. Pilot S/C Jean Gisclon. The white fuselage stripe was perhaps painted slightly before the attack on the French fleet at Mers-el-Kébir; this group was one of those which intervened against British aircraft, having first been de-militarised and then very urgently got airworthy again.

Curtiss H-75 A-3 N°249 from the *4e Escadrille* of GC II/5. Casablanca, Morocco, 1941. Pilot: A/C R. Delannoy. The separation between the colours is higher up than usual and is one of the features of planes in this unit. GC II/5 was the only one of the two French fighter squadrons to intervene over Mers-el-Kébir in July 1940 and indeed confront enemy aircraft. After the Armistice, the planes in the 3rd Flight were numbered from 1 to 12 and those in the 4th rom 14 to 25.

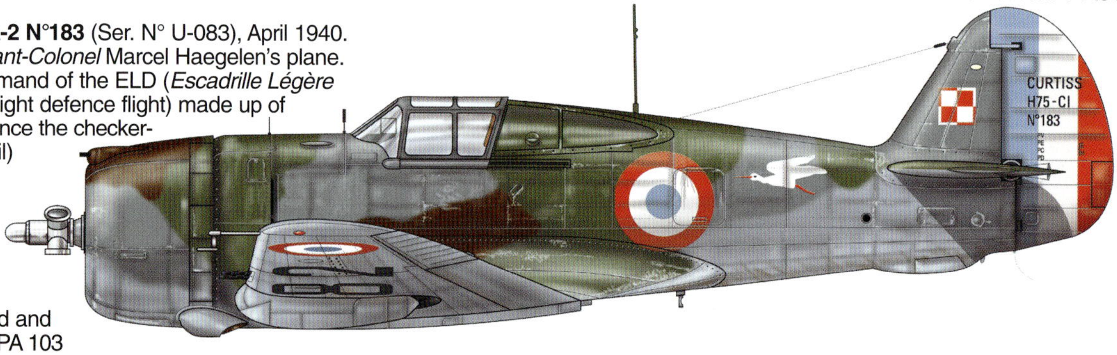

Curtiss H-75 A-2 N°183 (Ser. N° U-083), April 1940. This is *Lieutenant-Colonel* Marcel Haegelen's plane. He was in command of the ELD (*Escadrille Légère de Défense* – Light defence flight) made up of Polish pilots (hence the checker-board on the tail) entrusted with defending the SNAC factories at Le Bourget where H-75s were assembled and repaired. The SPA 103 stork on the fuselage recalls the flight in which this ace with 22 kills served during WWI.

THOSE THAT NEVER WERE...

Bloch MB 135

The 1934 fast bomber B4 programme which gave rise to the Amiot 351/354 and LeO 451 was considerably delayed and the next programme (1936), which accepted four-engined aircraft, turned out simply to be an amendment to the earlier one. On this occasion, several prototypes appeared, like the Breguet 482, or the CAO 700 (cf page 81) as well as the Bloch MB 134 or MB 135. All these machines were in the end included in the 'B4-multi-engined' (B4 – Bomber, four crew members) programme started in 1938.

At the end of 1936 the Bloch Company, now incorporated into the SNCASO , had thought of modernising its MB 131 (see page 31) by replacing the engines which were not powerful enough with Hispano-Suiza 14 AAs. This resulted in the creation of the **MB 133** with a twin tail assembly, which only flew in October 1937 because of the delays caused by the nationalisation of the armament industry. It was quickly followed by the **MB 134** fitted with the same wings and to all appearances identical to the 133, even if there were actually very few parts in common. This twin-engined plane, powered by Gnôme-Rhône 14P engines, was redesigned during the studies and resulted in a machine which was very close to the MB 174. A contract for three prototypes was signed and the first of them took to the air in July 1939. Although powered by the same engines as its competitors – GR 14N-48/49s – the machine turned out to be faster. After some modifications (bigger tail fins), this prototype was sent to the CEMA in January 1940. It was damaged in an accident and finally destroyed a few weeks later with the arrival of the Germans. Ever since the start of the MB 134 design

Bloch had been studying a four-engined version which for the period was unusual since twin-engined machines were much more popular in most countries. Compared with its running-mate, the new plane - the logically designated **MB 135** (of which only one of the two prototypes ordered was eventually built) - differed in its central wing section which was to take the four Gnôme-Rhône 14Ms. These were less powerful individually than the GR 14Ps of the twin-engined aircraft but their cross-section was narrower. With its wider oval fuselage which still had a step in which the rear gunner was positioned, and its bomb bay placed like on the MB 174 (cf page 45) between the two main wing longerons, this four-engined plane resembled the MB 162 (see below) although there was actually no relation between them. Powered by GR-14 M-6s on the left and M-7s on the right, each propeller rotating in the opposite direction to counterbalance the torque, the MB 135 took off for the first time at Villacoublay on 12 January 1939. It was a promising plane, easy to handle and performing at least as well as the LeO 451. In the end there was no series production; the authorities preferred to concentrate bomber production around the Amiot 351/354 and LeO 451 rather than risk spreading it too thin by building a third series of multi-engined aircraft.

TECHNICAL SPECIFICATIONS

Type
Four-seat bomber
Power Plant
Four 14-cylinder Gnôme-Rhône 14 M-6/7 air-cooled radials rated at 700 bhp at take-off.
Dimensions
Length: *50 ft 11 in.*
Height: *12 ft 10 in.*
Wingspan: *70 ft 3 in.*
Wing Area: *645.780 sq ft.*
Unladen Weight: *12,848 lb.*
Max. Weight: *25,265 lb.*
Performance
Max. Speed: *312 mph at 16 500 feet.*
Cruising Speed: *265 mph*
Range: *1 250 miles.*
Ceiling: *32 800 ft.*
Armament:
One flexible 7.5-mm MAC 34 machine gun in the nose; one 20-mm Hispano-Suiza canon in the dorsal position; one 7.5-mm MAC 34 machine gun in the ventral position; 2 970 lb of bombs.

Bloch MB 162

In 1937, Bloch threw himself into the design of two variants of his four-engined commercial aircraft, the MB 160, specially designed to serve on African air routes: the **MB 161** with a twin tail, larger wings, 900 bhp GR 14N engines and a fuselage modified to carry 33 passengers; and the long-haul **MB 162** with a narrower fuselage and designed to carry out flights over 4 375 miles. The estimated performances of the second machine were so encouraging that it was decided to transform it into a B5 (five crew members) bomber. A full-sized model of the machine was shown at the 1938 Salon de l'Aéronautique; it was powered by four HS 14 A4-12/13s rated at 1 100 bhp each. As priority had been given to the MB 161, construction of the MB 162 prototype (N°01) only started in 1939 and assembly followed in the following spring. It was an all-metal plane, with a monocoque fuselage and typically Bloch-style wings with their two transversal spars. Its armament included among other weapons two 20-mm cannon. The prototype flew for the first time on 1 June 1940 and was quickly ferried from Villacoublay to Bordeaux where the Germans eventually seized it. Trials continued in Luftwaffe colours in 1942 then the MB 162 N°01 was sent to Germany. It finished its career there in I./KG 200.

TECHNICAL SPECIFICATIONS

Type
Bomber with 5 crew members.
Power Plant
Four 14-cylinder Gnôme-Rhône 14N-48/49 air-cooled radials rated at 1100 bhp at take-off.
Dimensions
Length: *71 ft 10 in.*
Height: *12 ft 4 in.*
Wingspan: *106 ft 9 in.*
Wing Area: *1 162.404 sq ft.*
Unladen Weight: *26 070 lb.*
Max. Weight: *41 756 lb.*
Performance
Max. Speed: *344 mph at 16 500 ft.*
Range: *875 miles.*
Ceiling: *29 700 ft.*
Armament:
One flexible 7.5-mm MAC 34 machine gun in the nose, one 20-mm Hispano-Suiza canon in the dorsal position, another one and a flexible 7.5-mm machine gun in the ventral position; 7 920 lb of bombs carried internally.

Bloch MB 700

Among the manufacturers which replied to the tender for the 1936 programme for a light fighter built from non-strategic materials were Caudron (C.713), Arsenal (VG 30) and the SNCASO with its Bloch MB 700. The realisation of the project was given to André Herbemont. He was the designer of all the Blériot aircraft of the post WWI era. The company, like the 'Avions Marcel Bloch', had been incorporated into the nationalised company (SNCASO) at the end of 1936. The aircraft was made entirely of wood; it had a one-piece wing with two spars and the forward fuselage was covered with moulded plywood, the aft with fabric. The engine, a Gnôme-Rhône 14 M-6, was not exactly very powerful (700 bhp on take-off) but its estimated performance must have been quite honourable given its reduced mass. Even a carrier-borne version was planned. It is not known why, but the sole MB 700 prototype which flew for the first time, unarmed, on 19 April 1940 was not ferried to safety at the time of the German advance. The Germans, thinking it was booby-trapped, set fire to it when they discovered it on the airfield at Buc…

TECHNICAL SPECIFICATIONS

Type
Single-seat fighter
Power Plant
One 14-cylinder Gnôme-Rhône 14 M-6 air-cooled radial engine rated at 700 bhp at take-off.
Dimensions
Length: *24 ft 3 in.*
Height: *11 ft 3 in.*
Wingspan: *29 ft 5 in.*
Wing Area: *133.461 sq ft.*
Loaded Weight: *4 070 lb.*
Performance
Max. Speed: *344 mph at 13 200 ft (estimated).*
Range: *2 hours.*
Armament:
Two 20-mm Hispano-Suiza HS 404 cannon and two 7.5-mm MAC 34 machine guns in the wings.

Breguet 482

The A.21 Technical Programme dated December 1936 for B4 twin-engined aircraft powered by Gnôme-Rhône engines gave rise to two four-engined aircraft: the Bloch MB 135 and the **Breguet 482**. This machine itself came from the twin-engined Br 481 and Br 482 'raid' projects which were finally abandoned, before being built, in favour of the four-engined version with a reduced wing area and powered by Hispano-Suiza 12 Y-20/21s. Two prototypes of this machine were ordered on 12 May 1938 but building only started a year later; the power plants were changed (1 100 bhp HS 12 Y-0/51s) in the meantime. This very promising four-engined aircraft was made entirely of metal with a monocoque oval fuselage, the central part of the wing being integral with the fuselage and carrying the inboard engine nacelles. When they were almost finished, the two prototypes were evacuated at the end of May 1940, N°01 to Bône (Algeria) and N°02 to Anglet, near Biarritz. The first was eventually destroyed during the Allied landings in French North Africa and the second was stocked during the German occupation and eventually flew for the first time at Toulouse in November 1947 after completion. It was then converted into a test-bed after all its armament was removed.

TECHNICAL SPECIFICATIONS

Type
Four-seat bomber
Power Plant
Four 12-cylinder Hispano-Suiza 12 Y-51 liquid-cooled in-line engines rated at 1 100 bhp on take-off.
Dimensions
Length: *61 ft 11 in.*
Height: *14 ft 6 in.*
Wingspan: *79 ft 10 in*
Wing Area: *725.426 sq ft.*
Unladen Weight: *20 803 lb.*
Max. Weight: *35 200 lb.*
Performance
Max. Speed: *328 mph at 16 500 ft.*
Range: *1 000 miles.*
Ceiling: *39 600 ft.*
Armament:
One flexible 735-mm MAC 34 machine gun in the nose; one 20-mm Hispano-Suiza canon in the dorsal position; two 7.5-mm MAC 34 machine guns on separate mounts in the ventral position; 5 500 lb of bombs in the bay.

CAO 200

The former Nieuport Company, incorporated into the SNCAO after the 1936 nationalisations developed the LN 161 to meet the C1 Fighter Programme specification which was eventually won by the Morane-Saulnier MS 405. The same design was used again with the new 1937-1938 C1 Programme in which the Dewoitine D. 520 and the MS 450 took part. A full-sized model of the new machine, designated CAO 200, was shown at the 1938 Salon de l'Aéronautique. Building this machine used modern techniques, the electrically-welded structure being for example covered with Duralumin; the leading edges were fitted with slats and the incidence of the elevators could be varied. It was to have been fitted with a 1 100 bhp Hispano-Suiza 12 Y-51 engine, but the prototype finally flew with only an 830 bhp HS 12 Y-31 engine. During the following trials, various modifications were carried out, like using ejector exhaust stubs enabling an extra 10 mph or so to be gained. Extra vertical surfaces were added to the horizontal tail surfaces. Although the plane was under-powered and despite the fact that at the end of the tests the D.520

was ordered, the SNCAO was permitted to continue the experiments with twelve pre-series machines, none of which were ever finished. The prototype carried on with its experiments so as to perfect the pre-series machines and was even used in the last weeks of the Battle of France to protect the Villacoublay site. On one occasion its pilot, a civilian, managed to shoot down an enemy aircraft (a Heinkel 111) on 24 May 1940!

TECHNICAL SPECIFICATIONS

Type
Single-seat fighter
Power Plant
One 12-cylinder Hispano-Suiza Y-31 liquid-cooled engine rated at 860 bhp on take-off.
Dimensions
Length: *29 ft 4 in.*
Height: *11 ft 6 in.*
Wingspan: *31 ft 4 in.*
Wing Area: *143.148 sq ft*
Loaded Weight: *5 500 lb.*
Performance
Max. Speed: *344 mph at 19800 ft.*
Range: *2 hours.*
Ceiling: *36 300 ft.*
Armament:
One engine-mounted 20-mm Hispano-Suiza canon and two 7.5-mm MAC 34 machine guns in the wings.

CAO 700

Designed to meet the 1937 A20 Programme specifications for heavy multi-engined bombers carrying a crew of five, the **CAO 700** never left the ground because of the May-June 1940 events. The SNCAO - to which the Ateliers et Chantiers de la Loire were now incorporated - project used the **LN 10** (a two-seat seaplane) fuselage to which was added a new wing which housed four Gnôme-Rhône 14N-49 engines, which were identical to the starboard LeO 451 engine. This fuselage had a rectangular cross-section and was entirely made of metal. It housed an 18 ft 10 in long bomb bay displaced to port to leave space for a walkway. Extra projectiles (two 550-lb bombs) could be housed in the bays situated between the inboard engine nacelle and the fuselage. The crew consisted of a pilot and co-pilot sitting in tandem, a bombardier-navigator installed in the large glazed nose manning a 7.5-mm machine gun, a rear gunner in a SAMM turret armed with a 20-mm Hispano-Suiza canon and finally a radio operator in a compartment in the lower fuselage serving a pair of 7.5-mm rear defensive machine guns. This four-engined plane was ready to be assembled when the Germans approached St-Nazaire, so it was shipped by rail to Istres where several ground tests were carried out. By one of those quirks of fate, it was getting ready to take off on its first flight, crew in place and engines ticking over when the announcement of the Armistice grounded this very promising plane for ever…

At the time several derivatives had been envisaged, like the **CAO 700M** maritime reconnaissance aircraft, the **CAO 710** heavy bomber, a variant which used the fuselage of the 700 but with an increased wingspan and more powerful engines (GR 14 R-4/5 rated at 1 320 bhp) driving bigger propellers; and the **CAO 720** which could carry 15 passengers in a pressurized fuselage. It was 60% finished but the Germans forbade its completion.

TECHNICAL SPECIFICATIONS

Type
Bomber with 5 crew members
Power Plant
Four 14-cylinder Gnôme-Rhône 14 N-19 air-cooled radials engines rated at 1 140 bhp on take-off.
Dimensions
Length: *92 ft.*
Wingspan: *82 ft 3 in.*
Wing Area: *937.995 sq ft.*
Unladen Weight:
25 025 lb.
Max. Weight: *39 600 lb.*
Performance (Estim.)
Max. Speed: 337 mph at 17 490 ft.
Armament:
One flexible 7.5-mm MAC 34 machine gun in the nose; one 20-mm Hispano-Suiza canon in the dorsal turret; two 7.5-mm MAC in the ventral position.

Caproni Ca.313

Although France in its desire to find new, modern machines quickly turned to the USA at the end of the thirties, it was however looking elsewhere and was also interested in Italian production and in particular what the Italian firm, Caproni, was producing. Several orders were placed after the beginning of WWII of which only one was actually completed and then in hardly an effective way since out of the 200 Capronis ordered at the end of September 1939, only five examples were ever delivered before the June 1940 Armistice and especially before Italy's entry into the war. The story of this machine went back to 1936 and to the Ca. 309 Ghibli which gave rise to a very prolific line of twin-engined 'jack-of-all-trade' planes (their official designation RPB meant *Reconnaissance, Patrouille et Bombardement* -Reconnaissance, Patrol and Bombing – and even torpedo-dropping trials were carried out) which were amongst the planes the *Regia Aeronautica* used most, with 1 693 machines of all versions produced. The prototype of the Ca. 313, one of the last variants made its first flight in August 1939 but it entered service late because of difficulties encountered with the new Isotta in-line engines which were more powerful (700 bhp instead of 430 bhp) than the Ca.311's (the previous version) radials. This twin-engined plane had a very largely glazed fuselage (as it was to be used as a reconnaissance plane), was made of wood, canvas and light metal and could carry up to 880 lb of bombs internally but normally a spare fuel tank was installed instead.

The Armée de l'Air had thought of using the Ca. 313 RPB2 in its A3E (*Eclaireurs Triplaces* – three-seat scout plane) programme, to be attached to the medium bomber groups; these little, light and manoeuvrable twin-engined planes were to be used to scout for the other planes in their group. As has already been stated, only five of these machines were in fact delivered before the Armistice and none was used operationally. The planes were most likely recovered by the Italians and the Germans who were the other users of this type.

TECHNICAL SPECIFICATIONS

Type
Twin-engined three-seat Reconnaissance Bomber.
Power Plants
Two V-12 air-cooled Isotta-Fraschini RC 35 engines rated at 700 bhp.
Dimensions
Length: *38 ft 11 in.*
Height: *12 ft 2 in.*
Wingspan: *54 ft 11 in.*
Wing Area: *421.909 sq ft.*
Unladen Weight: *10120 lb.*
Weight Loaded: *12 980 lb.*
Performance
Max. Speed: *272 mph at 16 520 ft.*
Range:
750 miles.
Practical Ceiling:
24 090 ft.
Armament
Three 7.7-mm machine guns and 880 lb of bombs.

Abbreviations and Glossary

ANF: *Ateliers du Nord de la France*
BCR : *Bombardement, Chasse, Reconnaissance* (programme) - Bomber, Fighter, Reconnaissance.
Br : Breguet
CAO : shortened abbreviation for SNCAO (see SNCAO)
CEMA : *Centre d'Expérimentation du Materiel Aerien* – Air Equipment Experimental Centre.
CIB : *Centre d'Instruction au Bombardement* – Bomber Training Centre.
CIC: *Centre d'Instruction à la Chasse* – Fighter Training Centre.
CR : Caudron Renault.
DIAP : *Dépôt d'Instruction de l'Aviation Polonaise* – Polish Air Force Training depot.
EAA : *Etablissement de l'Armée de l'Air* – Air Force Establishment.
ECMJ : *Escadrille de Chasse Multiplace de Jour* –Day fighter flight (for multi-seat fighters)
ECN : *Escadrille de Chasse de Nuit* – Night-fighter flight.
ELD : *Escadrille Légère de Défense* – Light defence flight.
ERC : *Escadrille Régionale de Chasse* – Regional Fighter Flight.
Escadre (equiv. of the English Wing) : normally includes two *Groupes* or sometimes three. Originally, the fighter wings were numbered 1 to 10, the bombers from 11 to 20, observation from 31 to 40, reconnaissance from 51 to 60. This order was modified in view of the successive dissolution and creation of units.
Escadrille (equiv. Flight): the basic unit consisting of nine planes in theory for the fighters, divided into three patrols of three aircraft. Most *escadrilles* had a specific insignia, often inherited from a WWI unit whose traditions it has taken up. The first *Groupe* regroups the 1st and 2nd *Escadrilles*, the second the 3rd and 4th and the third the 5th and 6th. However one can sometimes also find that the *1re Escadrille* of GC II/1 is in fact the 3rd of *Groupe* 1
GAA : *Groupe Aérien Autonome.*
GAO: *Groupe Aérien d'Observation* – Air Observation Squadron (replaced GAR in September 1939.
GAR : *Groupe Aérien Régional* - Regional Air Squadron.
GARC : *Groupe Aérien Régional de Chasse* – Regional Air Fighter Squadron.
GB : *Groupe de Bombardement* – Bomber squadron.
GC : *Groupe de Chasse* – Fighter squadron.
GR : *Groupe de Reconnaissance* – reconnaissance squadron.
GR : Gnôme et Rhône (engines).
Groupe (equiv. Squadron) : composed of 2, sometimes 3 *escadrilles*. Each *Groupe* was identified by a Roman number indicating its position and an Arabic figure indicating the Group. Thus GB I/21 is the 1st *Groupe* (Squadron) of the *21e Escadre* (Wing), regrouping the *1re* and *2e Escadrilles* (Flights).
HS : Hispano-Suiza (engines and cannon).
LeO: Lioré et Olivier
LN: Loire Nieuport
MAC: Manufacture d'Armes de Chatellerault
MB: (Avions) Marcel Bloch
MS: Morane Saulnier
NiD: Nieuport Delage
SAB: Société Aéronautique Bordelaise
SAL: Salmson, the name of the plane used by the escadrille during WWI.
SECM: Société d'Emboutissage et de Construction Mécanique
SNCAC: Société Nationale de Construction d'Avions du Centre
SNCAN: Société Nationale de Construction d'Avions du Nord
SNCAO: Société Nationale de Construction d'Avions de l'Ouest
SNCASE: Société Nationale de Construction d'Avions du Sud Est
SNCASO: Société Nationale de Construction d'Avions du Sud Ouest
SPA: Spad , the name of the plane used by the escadrille during WWI
ZOA: *Zone d'Opérations Aériennes* – Air Operations Zone and by extension **ZOAN** (*Nord* –North), ZOAE (*Est*- East), etc..

SUFFIXES

(added after the designation of the plane) and indicating its use (e.g. MS 406 C1)

A2/A3: Observation, two/three seater.
A3E: Scout plane, three seats
AB2: Two –seat assault/attack bomber.
B2/B3/B4/B5: Bomber, 2, 3, 4, 5 crew members.
C1/C2/C3: Fighter, single 2 or 3 seater.
Ent: *Entraînement* – Training/trainer.
M (5): Multi Seater Bomber (5 crew members).
N (ou n): Night - CN *Chasse de nuit*: night fighter
BN : *Bombardement de nuit* – night bomber.
Example: BN5 : Night bomber, five crew members.
R2B2: Two-seat Reconnaissance Bomber.

Selected Bibliography

– « Amiot 350, LeO 45 et autres B4. R. Cuny & J. Danel. Docavia. Ed. Larivière.
– « *Bloch MB 151 & 152* ». Profile n° 201.
– « Le *Bloch 152* ». S. Joanne. Lela Presse
– « *Le Curtiss H-75 et ses dérivés* ». R. Cuny & G. Beauchamp. Docavia. Ed. Larivière.
– « *Invisibles Vainqueurs* ». J. & P. Martin. Cl. Michelet Ed.
– « *Ils étaient là...* ». J. & P. Martin. Aéro Editions.
– « Le grand livre des chasseurs ». W. Green & G. Swanborough. Celiv
– « Les avions ». E. Angelucci & P. Matricardi. Elsevier.
– Encyclopédie Mach 1
– Articles in the following magazines: *Aéro Journal, Avions, Fana de l'Aviation, Icare, Réplic, Scale Aicraft Modeller, Scale Aviation Modelling.*

Design and Lay-out by Dominique BREFFORT, André JOUINEAU and Antoine POGGIOLI, © *Histoire & Collections 2004.*

ISBN: 2-915239-23-1

Publisher's number: 2-915239
© Histoire & Collections 2004

Un ouvrage édité par
HISTOIRE & COLLECTIONS
SA au capital de 182 938, 82 €

5, avenue de la République
F-75541 Paris Cedex 11
Téléphone: 01 40 21 18 20
Fax: 01 47 00 51 11

This book has been designed, typed, laid-out and processed by *'Le Studio Graphique Armes & Collections'* fully integrated computer equipment.

Printed by ECGI
Spain, European Union
october 2004